DANCE MARATHONS

PERFORMANCE STUDIES
Expressive Behavior in Culture

Sally Harrison-Pepper, General Editor

Dance Marathons

PERFORMING AMERICAN CULTURE
OF THE 1920S AND 1930S

Carol Martin

Foreword by Brooks McNamara

UNIVERSITY PRESS OF MISSISSIPPI
Jackson

Manufactured in the United States of America

97 96 95 94   4 3 2 1

The paper in this book meets the guidelines for permanence and durability of
the Committee on Production Guidelines for Book Longevity of the Council on
Library Resources.

Library of Congress Cataloging-in-Publication Data

Martin, Carol J.
    Dance marathons : performing American culture of the 1920s and 1930s /
Carol Martin ; foreword by Brooks McNamara.
        p.   cm. — (Performance studies, expressive behavior in culture)
    Includes bibliographical references (p.   ) and index.
    ISBN 0-87805-673-4. — ISBN 0-87805-701-3 (pbk.)
        1. Dance marathons—United States—History. 2. Dance marathons—
Social aspects—United States. 3. United States—Social life and customs—
1918–1945. I. Title. II. Series.
    GV1623.M37   1994
    792.8—dc20   94-12157
                                                                    CIP

British Library Cataloging-in-Publication data available

For my mother, father, and grandmother

who knew those times

Contents

Illustrations

Foreword

Carol Martin's book is an intriguing account of the development of marathon dancing in America. But what kind of book is it, after all? Perhaps the best way to suggest what lies behind it is to mention what I see as the three most important influences on Martin's work—the development of popular entertainment research, feminist theory, and the growth of performance studies. I don't believe I overstate the case very much when I suggest that a quarter of a century ago writing about theatre and dance was hermetically sealed—that the reference points were almost all within the forms themselves. What actor or dancer did this? What company did that? What was the design like? What was the critical reception?

For the most part, at that time, working within an essentially closed form represented the only acceptable approach for historians of the performing arts. Among theatre scholars, for example, there was a conviction that throughout history there had been some sort of performance hierarchy that ranged from "greatest artistic achievements" to charming but basically inconsequential works in the folk and popular idioms.

But gradually that emphasis began to change—in part as a result of the growth of interest in popular entertainment. By the mid-seventies it was apparent that this new field, in spite of old biases, was starting to emerge as a viable alternative for historians. Conferences on entertainment were held in England and America. A number of books, articles, and journals were beginning to take up issues related to popular material. Behind all of the discussions, lay a fundamental question: If art is not the chief issue in discussing much of popular entertainment, what *is* the issue? Perhaps, many of us thought, it is its relationship to the culture that produced it. In fact, this seemed to be a logical answer; at any moment in history popular entertainment invariably seems to confront what is on people's minds with extraordinary directness and clarity.

There was another important resource, however, in that then *rara avis* performance studies. As it developed at New York University some twenty-five years ago—and more recently elsewhere—performance studies came to insist that the theatre is merely one of many forms that have always made up a larger phenomenon—performance. Beyond that, from the beginning, performance studies has never emphasized literary texts or the so-called "great achievements" in performance, but instead has always placed strong emphasis on other kinds of texts, on comparative relationships between forms of performance, and on the relationships between performances and the cultures that produced them. As a result, the emerging performance studies approach began to provide theatre and dance historians with new ways to understand popular entertainment.

Within the discipline of performance studies, however, different theoretical perspectives began to emerge. Very important was the development of feminist theory. Thus, while treating dance marathons as cultural texts, Martin has used feminist theory to expose the ways in which interactions are predicated on gender.

My point is simply that this "braid" of influences from popular entertainment, feminist theory, and performance studies has had more impact than we may realize; the braid has certainly influenced the work of many younger scholars, whose options now include an increasing number of new tasks and new subjects. Among them is Carol Martin.

How does one define Martin's *Dance Marathons*, then? Perhaps most clearly by the subtitle: *Performing American Culture of the 1920s and 1930s*. The book is filled with fascinating insights into the technical details of dance marathons. But it is probably best defined by the fact that it portrays dance marathons as an integral part of an increasingly troubled America in the late twenties and early thirties. Martin's book is part of a growing, vigorous scholarly movement that is exploring the history of amusements, theatre, dance, and other forms of live performance, not mostly as art forms, good or bad, but as central documents of cultures that created them.

Brooks McNamara
New York University

Acknowledgments

Anyone who writes about performance is indebted to the people who make performances. It is a pleasure to be able to name a few of the many thousands who participated in dance marathons and who have shared with me how they danced, sang, entertained, watched, and promoted them: Rajah Bergman, Norma Jasper, Edna Smith, Betty Freund, Everett Perlman, Betty Herndon Meyer, George Cook, and John Meehan. In addition, Richard Elliott, Stan West, and most of all George Eells have been especially helpful. Eells has been most generous with his knowledge, insights, and photographs.

Barbara Kirshenblatt-Gimblett, Cynthia Novak, Michael Kirby, and Cynthia Ward all read and commented on an early draft of this manuscript. Brooks McNamara has been a formidable mentor who has read and commented on both early and later drafts. McNamara's knowledge of popular culture and belief in my work have been a sustaining influence. Thomas Kessner, who led the 1991 National Endowment for the Humanities Summer Seminar for College Teachers, *The Making of Modern America,* offered many useful suggestions, as did the participants in that seminar. My participation in the seminar, in which I continued my research for this book, was funded by an NEH Summer Seminar Fellowship.

A number of people have aided me in the preparation of the manuscript: they include Bill Doyle, Radz Subramanium, Lauren Sherman, and Lys Ann Shore. I am also indebted to Sharon Mazer, Ann Daly, and Susan Ware for commenting on different chapters. Richard Schechner has made invaluable suggestions and has remained enthusiastic and supportive throughout this project. My sister Claudia Teich has shared the pleasure of the completion of this book.

I also wish to thank Sally Harrison-Pepper, the series editor, and JoAnne Prichard, the executive editor of the University Press of Mississippi, for their comments and support.

Introduction

When on September 24, 1993, President Bill Clinton appeared on television to explain his national health plan, he promised to answer in detail every single question put to him by the studio audience assembled to simulate a town meeting. Maureen Dowd, on special assignment for the *New York Times,* noted that the president's promise to tell all "alarmed his staff members, who envisioned the policy equivalent of the dance-marathon movie *They Shoot Horses, Don't They?*" Why is the seemingly endless, round-the-clock entertainment of the 1920s and 1930s still alive enough in the public imagination to characterize the behavior of someone in 1993? Dowd did not have to explain to her readers what a dance marathon was; she knew they would understand exactly what the president's staff feared.

Dance marathons still have a hold on the imagination of the American public not only because of the notoriety they attracted during the Great Depression, but also because they seem to epitomize the "American dream" in one of its crazier and more contradictory manifestations. Marathons signaled grit and hope, determination and foolishness, flimflam and patriotic bunting, athleticism and a wild mix of musical numbers, good clean fun and off-color jokes, nice "boys and girls" and prostitution, tireless endurance and utter exhaustion. Few Americans in 1993 can recall these events directly. Most people know of them through a popular 1969 movie starring Jane Fonda, *They Shoot Horses, Don't They?* The film was based on a 1935 novel of the same name written by Horace McCoy, who worked as a bouncer at several marathons in California. The Fonda film acquainted a whole new generation of Americans with dance marathons—or at least with Hollywood's interpretation of McCoy's version of a fictional dance marathon.

Almost everyone "knows" about dance marathons, yet today almost no one knows about them in any verifiable detail. These endurance entertainments have floated in the popular imagination unanchored by historical detail or critical study. Until now, McCoy's novel and the film have stood in for actual documentation and analysis. McCoy's version of marathons portrays tawdry events that cruelly exploit young people already beat up by the Depression. This is most vividly shown in the final scene of the movie, when Fonda's character asks her partner to shoot her.

They Shoot Horses, Don't They? is a fictional account driven by McCoy's desire to gain recognition as an American existentialist writer. There is little awareness, except among surviving professionals, that marathons were actually extremely complicated performative events. In appearance they were modeled on a radical version of social Darwinism, where the fittest would not just survive but triumph and win cash prizes. Although they appeared to be a contest among hopeful amateurs, marathons actually mixed professional performers playing the roles of contestants with authentic amateurs. Sometimes the contestants knew the marathons were fixed, sometimes they did not. In either case, the contestants were just part of the show. Masters of ceremonies (emcees) and celebrities, big-name singers and newcomers trying to make a name, worked alongside former vaudeville comedians looking for employment as vaudeville went under. The whole event was accompanied by bands or victrolas blaring the popular dance music of the period—jazz tunes, foxtrots, lindys, and the charleston. The bands and major entertainers appeared only during prime time, the 8 p.m. show. At other times, the marathon arenas were populated by second-string emcees, floor judges, a scattering of spectators, and the bedraggled contestants.

Surprisingly for a phenomenon so vividly present in the American imagination, and so complexly expressing American values, dance marathons have not been the subject of much serious scholarly study. Most of what has been written is anecdotal and poorly documented. In their heyday, dance marathons were among America's most widely attended and controversial forms of live entertainment. The business employed an estimated 20,000 people as promoters, masters of ceremonies, floor judges, trainers, nurses, and contestants. There were many times that number of spectators, although no reliable attendance estimates were ever made. Marathons were performed in coliseums, armories, dance halls, and tents. The venues ranged in size from small local halls with audiences of 200 or 300 to coliseums seating as many as 5,000. Exactly how many U.S. cities and towns hosted dance marathons is not known, but my research indicates that the number must be in the thousands. Almost all cities with populations of 50,000 or more held at least one marathon. Thanks to the promoter Hal J. Ross, dance marathons were also performed in Europe as an extension and simulation of American culture.

Of course, marathons also stirred opposition. Moralists and "church ladies" as well as the police wanted to strictly regulate and ultimately extinguish this form of "dangerous" (sexual, licentious, connected to criminal activities) entertainment. Movie theater owners, recognizing that marathons posed stiff competition for scarce Depression dollars, also wanted the endurance shows stifled.

Where did the concept of marathons originate? There is some indication that endurance entertainment similar to dance marathons was not uncommon during the 19th century. In Harry Helms' scrapbook in the Houdini collection in the Library of Congress there is a description of a "continuous" medicine show. The continuous event was a walking contest for which a track was built around the perimeter of the seats. The laps were posted on a blackboard, specialty numbers were performed every hour, and a prize was offered to the winner.

The idea, of course, harks back to classical Greek civilization and the long footrace from Marathon to Athens. The modern Olympics had its première in 1896. The event focused public attention on a variety of sports contests that emphasized competition among nations as well as individuals striving to set "world records." Such high-minded events were controlled by strict codes of participation. They were far from being universal contests open to all. The Olympics initially welcomed only the "best youth"—those young people who were rich or supported by upper-class civic organizations, specially trained, and white. Nevertheless, the Olympic games inspired many offshoots, both professional and parodic. After World War I drew into its deathly maw young men of all social classes, the population of "ordinary people" began more and more to participate in their own version of Olympic-style and professional sports competitions.

From the first, the word *marathon* was used to characterize these contests of endurance dancing. Dance marathons began in the 1920s as part of the craze to break world records. By the mid-1930s they had become an extended form of entertainment. If the records of the world-class athletes were beyond the dreams of ordinary persons, the promise of fame and perhaps wealth was still possible through endurance contests.

The dance marathon phenomenon can be divided into three phases. The first was the outburst of hourly dance contests in the spring of 1923. Then, between 1923 and 1928, dance marathons changed from hourly endurance contests to entertainment spectacles. Finally, from 1929 to 1934, as the Depression deepened, the endurance contests came to display the full panoply of characteristics that still marks them in the public imagination.

The first phase consisted simply of nonstop dancing to live music. This kind of display could hardly make an entertainment. Nonstop dancing was boring to watch; it mattered only to distant newspaper readers and a few friends of the contestants who came to urge them on. This initial phase of marathon dancing was part of the craze for flagpole sitting, mountain climbing, long-distance airplane flights, and the like that swept postwar America and Europe. This kind of impetuous entrepreneurship was difficult to exploit commercially on a regular basis. Nevertheless, entertainment and sports promoters saw the possibility of money to be made in promoting marathon dancing. Unlike flagpole sitting, marathons had action; unlike long-distance plane flights, marathons took place where a crowd could sit and watch. A whole range of special attractions could be positioned around the central event of an endurance dance contest. If the home-town aspect of dance marathons could be professionalized with specialty entertainments, spectators would pay good money to see such shows. They might even keep paying around the clock—more during prime time, less late at night and during the day.

The second phase of marathons culminated in 1928 with a show at Madison Square Garden in New York City. In this phase rules were developed to govern the whole event. A spectacle sharing characteristics of both athletic competition and theater was emerging. Rules specified dancing time and rest periods. Generally forty-five minutes of dancing was followed by fifteen minutes of rest, twenty-four hours a day.

The dance hall was partitioned into a dance competition area, places for the band and other entertainers, resting places and medical quarters (often in full view of the spectators), and offstage control and supply centers. Marathons included emcees, floor judges, an orchestra, entertainers, nurses, food providers, hawkers of souvenirs and snacks for the spectators, and special guests, as well as the dancers themselves. Of course, the arena was mostly given over to spectator seating. Ringside seats allowed spectators to interact with the dancers. Thus marathons developed into a complex event involving competition, drama, music, and other kinds of popular entertainment, as well as audience participation.

In the third phase of dance marathons, the shows evolved into Depression-era entertainment. The long hours of the contests reflected the amount of time spectators had on their hands. Unemployed, bored, and sometimes angry, spectators spent days and nights watching the "kids" make their endless rounds on the dance floor. Some of the better heeled spectators acted out their superiority by "spraying" the contestants with coins after specialty numbers. The competitors were no longer just amateurs who hoped to make some money, pass the time, gain public attention, and have fun. Instead, they were comprised of a mix of amateurs and professionals. The pros went from marathon to marathon, often following a particular promoter. Sometimes the promoters asked these contestants to participate in added entertainments like mock weddings (or real ones), fights, or specialty numbers. Other contestants stayed in the contest only long enough to milk it for food and a place to flop.

Actual entertainment and dramatic situations arose more or less spontaneously in earlier shows. These were then highlighted and professionalized during the Depression. Special entertainment features were added, and local celebrities often "dropped by" to say a few words of encouragement—or, given the cruelty of the times, disparagement—to the contestants. The live orchestra was spelled by phonograph music, and the audience was invited to dance during the fifteen-minute rest periods. In this third phase, marathons also became known as walkathons. Races and elimination features in which the contestants had to maintain some form of continual motion—usually a combination of dancing and walking—were incorporated into dance marathons.

By the 1930s marathons had assumed a particular shape. Because they were almost always organized from outside the town or city where they were held, the staging of a marathon often resembled an invasion (or infiltration). An advance man selected the locations for marathons. He often doubled as a publicity agent, contacting local business people and authorities. The advance man's job was to soften up a community, to line up important people behind the coming show, and to pepper the local press with enticing notices. The entire community could benefit from a well-attended marathon. Merchants could sell their wares at the marathon, and banners and billboards would advertise their stores' locations and goods. The advance man also dealt with the local police and the local laws governing the assembly of a large number of people, as well as regulations concerning how long a continuous-motion contest could last. The advance man arranged for whatever work was needed to spruce up an arena and make it suitable for a marathon. An orchestra platform, a public-address system, an infirmary, and rest quarters were needed, in addition to a raised rectangular dance floor. Seating had to be provided for the spectators. The logistical requirements of a marathon were closer to those of a circus than to those of a traveling Broadway show.

While the advance man was working in the town weeks ahead of time, the promoter was busy assembling his marathon team. Most important was the master of ceremonies, or emcee, a man who could elicit laughter and tears from the audience by playing on the situations he saw in front of him. Diplomatic floor judges were required, along with head trainers, nurses, and at least one medical doctor who could treat the injuries and ailments peculiar to the activity.

In terms of performance theory, dance marathons exemplified social Darwinism at the same time that they parodied and critiqued it. Much of the struggle and competition in marathons was rigged. As with professional wrestling today, spectators came to witness and enjoy the show, not to be taken in by its "authenticity." Everyone knew that much of what went on at marathons was theatricalized. This did not prevent the events from being emblematic of people's lives during the Depression. As the documentary expression of the period testifies in photographs like those of Walker Evans, survival was easily rendered in aesthetic terms. In marathons, the grind of endless though sometimes barely discernible movement, swollen feet, searing muscle pain, and utter exhaustion was set against blaring music, sprint racing, the sweet wailing of a jazz singer, or the "unexpected" appearance of a celebrity. Cunningly, the best promoters were able to orchestrate a mixture of real life—with its unpredictability, inconsistencies, and interruptions—and carefully contrived entertainments and "family dramas." The dramas included marriages, rivalries, spats, and brief romantic affairs enacted on the dance floor or in the rest areas. Dance marathons presented life lived as theater.

The "real life" aspect of marathons has been so exaggerated and mythologized that the shows' unique place in American popular entertainment has been largely overlooked. Theater is what enabled spectators to enjoy all the hours of what would otherwise have been unendurably boring dancing. Survival was indeed on display—but in quotation marks. Spectators simultaneously believed and disbelieved. It was a position Bertolt Brecht would have appreciated: the enjoyment of an aesthetic phenomenon only partly masked as a real-life event. Marathons combined the wholly staged, the partly staged, and the real. Successful shows depended on promoters who knew how to manipulate endless hours of dancing, which without clever theatrical framing would have been of little interest to an audience. Of course, the contestants experienced real exhaustion and pain, but ultimately the contests were a unique kind of theater—a combination of gladiatorial display and professional finesse.

It was the coupling of the "authentic" with the "staged" that made marathons so popular. Spectators came to see the contestants hurt. The eruption of actual pain in the midst of the contest created what must have been a pleasurable disjunction between the spectators' and the contestants' frames of reference. Especially during the Depression, spectators could displace their own misery onto the sheer physical pain of the participants. They felt a vicarious pleasure, bordering on sadism. At the same time the emcee, the band, and the entertainers reassured the spectators that it was all "make believe," that the boys and girls were really having fun, that everything was voluntary. Both messages were sent night after night, contest after contest: this is real, this is theater; these are people who are really suffering, these are people having fun. The theatrical aspect of marathons was always subverted by their brutish and cruel real-life qualities, just as the grueling marathon life was constantly modulated into (painless, harmless) theater. It was rather like seeing a stage fight erupt into a real fight and then realizing that the contestants were exaggerating their anger and their injuries for the sake of theatrical display.

Several factors led to the decline of marathons in the mid-1930s. As the Depression deepened, there was less and less money available. And although marathons were full entertainments, they were also fads. Unlike baseball, regular theater and dance, or popular music, marathons did not draw repeat audiences. Once people had been to one, that satisfied them. To put it another way, the repetition and boredom inherent in the genre overtook whatever theatrics were mixed into the contests. Unlike sports, marathons aroused little lasting interest about records set; there were no "marathon heroes" comparable to sports figures.

Further, marathons generated considerable opposition on both moral and economic grounds. Some people opposed marathons because they "corrupted" youth, especially young women. The police were suspicious of marathons because community sentiment was against such events. Besides, police officers did not welcome the extra hassle of monitoring a twenty-four-hour, seven-day-a-week entertainment. Movie theater operators opposed marathons because they were competing for the same leisure-time dollars. Because movie houses were permanent features in a community, their owners usually could count on the police and the local authorities to harass marathon promoters.

The promoters made efforts to regularize and organize their shows. The National Endurance Amusement Association (NEAA) was formed in 1935 to transform marathons into a legitimate business, but it actually signaled the hopelessness of the situation. When the marathon business was thriving, there was no need for a national organization. When the need arose, the promoters were too suspicious of one another for the organization to be effective. More than a few were dishonest men who resisted the notion of regulation. Promoters hunted around for "virgin towns" where they could stage shows and then move on. In its death throes, the NEAA threw open its membership to performers and contestants as well as promoters. Precious few joined.

In the late 1930s other events overtook the marathons. Long before December 7, 1941, American industry had begun to gear up for war. After Germany invaded Poland in 1939, bringing France and England into conflict with Germany for the second time in a generation, many people knew it was only a matter of time before the United States would be drawn into the war. Dance marathons had begun after World War I. They had emerged as an entertainment of striving and hope and then, with the Depression, had modulated into an entertainment of the desperate grind. But with another world war looming, American attitudes were shifting. Industry had revived, and people were going back to work. Who had the time to sit around for hours watching people move in a circle on a dance floor? Life had a purpose once again. Although some marathons persisted into the 1940s—at least one took place as late as 1952—their time of popularity was over. This form of entertainment was for all purposes dead.

In their own time, marathons were related not only to the record-breaking craze of the 1920s, an association the marathons outgrew. They were also linked to several kinds of emergent serial and on-the-spot entertainments. There were the popular movie serials, which consisted of short episodes rising to a horrific climax—often the impending death of the heroine or hero—interrupted at the precise moment before disaster. The next week's episode showed how in the nick of time, through clever action or propitious intervention, the heroine or hero escaped harm. The 1930s also saw the rise of the movie newsreel, in which the events of the day—usually a few weeks old—were graphically presented as "real-life drama." In the mid-1930s, under the sponsorship of the Federal Theatre Program, the "Living Newspaper" became very popular. The Living Newspaper combined theater, journalism, and the movie newsreel. Often staged in a multimedia fashion, it enacted events of the day in a simple, graphic manner. The tone of the Living Newspapers was often highly political, leaning to the left. Radio serials also came into their own in the 1930s. These programs featured daily episodes of stories that never ended. The heroines and heroes of the "soap operas" (as they were called because of their commercial sponsors) ranged from women struggling to make ends meet in a hard world to superheroes like Captain Midnight or Superman. All these entertainments shared with marathons the qualities of seriality, suspense, melodrama, and a free mixture of fantasy and actuality. Except for the Living Newspaper, these entertainments were, on the surface at least, apolitical; they tended to substantiate orthodox values and ideologies. Like dance marathons, these forms of popular culture attempted to negotiate social, political, and economic forces in performative terms easily understandable by average men and women.

In the decades since the demise of dance marathons, other entertainments have filled more or less the same niche in American popular culture. For example, roller derbies, popular in the 1940s and 1950s, grew out of dance marathons. The marathons had sometimes featured dancers on skates for a specialty number. Professional wrestling—today's dominant not-fake, not-real hard-body entertainment—also repeats many of the themes and traits of dance marathons. Wrestlers are divided into good guys and bad guys, and the spectators are enormously and passionately involved in their matches even though most of them know the outcome has been arranged, the falls rehearsed, and the screams and moans practiced. Each of these entertainments—soaps, Living Newspapers, newsreels, derbies, wrestling matches—could be analyzed in its own right to see what it would yield concerning American values and consciousness in performance.

In writing this book about dance marathons, I have worked mostly from primary source materials. I interviewed people who had danced in marathons, and I found marathon promoters and publicists and was able to examine their photographs and scrapbooks.

Many marathon dancers and entertainers ended up in Hollywood. A few became well known. But for each exceptional performer, such as June Havoc and Red Skelton, there were thousands of hangers-on who found a role here and there in the movies or worked as extras. The point is that many marathon contestants came to think of themselves as professional performers. They "discovered" their calling on the marathon dance floor. But the genre betrayed them. Those who did go on to bigger things, like Skelton, were already professionals when they began their marathon careers.

What happened to the promoters is less clear. Some may have tried promoting other types of events, such as boxing or wrestling matches. Others got out of show business altogether.

On a theoretical and critical level, my research into dance marathons asks one overarching question: what is the relationship between performance and the cultural moment in which it is produced? Although much history has been written about dance and theater, interpreting that history is not easy. My work on dance marathons both transcribes the history of these events and tries to interpret their meanings. I situate dance marathons within discourses of feminism, popular entertainments, performance theory, and American history.

This book begins by tracing the development of marathons from their first occurrence as hourly endurance dance contests in 1923 through their development into entertainment spectacles—with vaudeville sketches, weddings, mock weddings, ballroom dancing, and elimination features—during the Depression. At the heart of the book is an analysis of the complexity of the performative realities of marathons. This analysis leads to a discussion of the role of women at these events in the context of changing notions of gender. In an effort to better understand marathons from a promoter's point of view, I have devoted a chapter to promoter Hal J. Ross and the shows he staged in Texas and Florida. The final two chapters of the book discuss the attempt to legitimize marathons with the formation of the NEAA and the eventual decline of the entertainment.

My goal in writing this book was to document, discuss, and analyze a well-known but little-understood form of American popular culture. Although dance marathons are, as Dowd's allusion to them shows, very much alive in the popular imagination, what precisely they were is little known. Some think of dance marathons as nothing more than a Depression-era entertainment, a nihilistic poor-man's nightclub. But in truth they were much more than that. They were complex performance events that negotiated important cultural shifts and conflicts of American life between the world wars. Marathons collapsed the distance between real life and theater, reflecting a larger cultural obsession with celebrity, notoriety, endurance, and identity.

DANCE MARATHONS

One

COMMON HEROES

We turn casually to the day's news at breakfast with no
thought of acquiring a new hero on this particular morning, and in bold type spread the full width of a front page
find that a new hero has sprung full-panoplied from the
news like Minerva from the head of Jupiter. Some bold
deed performed lone-handed, some spectacular and un-
exampled feat, some service to a cause worthwhile but
hitherto quiescent, leaps out at us in giant headlines.

Charles Mertz, *The Great American Band Wagon:
A Study of Exaggerations* (1928)

In a nonstop flurry of foxtrot, one-step, and waltz, Alma Cummings set the first dance marathon record in the United States.
Beginning Saturday, March 30, 1923, at 6:57 p.m. and ending
Sunday, March 31, 1923, at 9:57 p.m., Cummings achieved her twenty-
seven-hour victory at the dingy Audubon Ballroom at 168th Street and
Broadway in New York and stole the record first established in Great
Britain. Her victory started a craze of record-breaking nonstop dancing
that received national attention for several months. These early dance
marathons and the breathless attention they received in the spring and
early summer of 1923 set the stage for the development of the dance
marathons of the Depression, which lasted for weeks and even months
at a time. They also foreshadowed the difficulty promoters and contestants would have in trying to make dance marathons a legitimate form
of popular entertainment.

The mood of the country in 1923 had changed greatly from the intensity of the World War I years. If national mood swings and values can be said to have a determining effect on the course of history, then the change in the sentiments of the country during this time helped determine at least the immediate future. "The hedonistic, greedy, self-centered norms of the twenties, which played no small part in the coming of the Depression, were at least intensified by the wrapping of the war in the mantle of progressive moralism."[1] Americans felt that they had paid their dues during the war and could now turn their attention to personal concerns. For an older generation, the optimism of the Progressive years gave way to a feeling of loss of the well-being they had experienced in the prewar years, flavored with the remnants of the patriotism of the war.[2] For a younger generation, Americanism had nothing to do with nostalgia. Instead, it took the form of freedom of expression in leisure activities.

In the process of setting her record, Cummings wore out six partners and several pairs of shoes. In Cummings's tireless grasp, young men wilted one after another. When the band stopped for the night, two phonographs furnished the music; when the crowds went home to sleep, ballroom proprietor George D. Grundy kept vigil with a few diehard patrons. For her part, Cummings just danced, all night and all day. The morning press heralded her victory as if it were the marker of a new kind of common hero.[3]

We have no idea what Cummings might have been thinking of as she danced, or what dancing might have meant to her. Was she really desirous of fame beyond the world she knew, or was she testing her limits on a lark? What we do know is that she was well prepared for her achievement. When the hour of her triumph arrived, the band, "which had slept, eaten, been to church, and returned," blared "The Star-Spangled Banner," thereby casting Cummings's accomplishment as something as uniquely American as the national anthem.[4] In those culminating moments, in spite of sweat, swollen feet, and muscle spasms in her legs, Cummings spun out to the middle of the dance floor and performed a whirlwind waltz with her final partner, twenty-year-old George Madaro. That the Audubon ballroom was littered with cigarette stubs and reeking with the smell of stale coffee and tobacco did not matter. For Alma Cummings the world was in motion, and for twenty-seven hours she was the center of its movement.

When she finally stopped dancing, thirty-two-year-old Alma modestly wrapped her legs with a towel and pulled up her skirt to soak her feet. With her feet in a basin of water Alma graciously answered reporters' questions and posed for a photograph holding up for the camera a pair of shoes with holes in the soles. She told the reporters her life story. She had been raised in a Catholic convent but had converted to Seventh-Day Adventism. Her success, she testified, was due to the healthful atmosphere of her native Texas and her nine-year vegetarian diet. "While dancing," Alma said, "I ate only fruit, nuts, and near beer." One *New York Times* journalist ironically noted that no matter how much of her success Alma attributed to her diet and the climate of her native Texas, it must be remembered that Madaro, who had danced seven hours, rested nine, and had then come back for the finish, was neither a Texan nor a vegetarian.[5]

Cummings established her record in the face of international competition. Twelve days earlier, on February 18, two dance teachers, Olie Finnerty and Edgar Van Ollefin from Sunderland, England, had danced for seven hours without stopping.[6] Following their achievement, records were set in Edinburgh (fourteen hours, thirty-six minutes), Marseilles (twenty-four hours, four minutes) and Paris (twenty-four hours, twenty minutes).[7] Cummings and ballroom proprietor Grundy were explicitly challenging England and bringing the passion for marathon dancing to the United States. No one could foresee that this fledgling endeavor would be the basis for a new form of entertainment that was alternately known as "endurance dance," "nonstop dance," "long distance dancing," "jitterathons," "speed derbies," "walkashows," "walkathons," and most commonly "dance marathons."

Dance marathons were part of a larger cultural discourse of the 1920s about breaking records. People would try almost anything on a dare. To win a five-hundred-dollar bet, Bill Williams of Hondo, Texas, spent thirty days pushing a peanut up Pike's Peak with his nose.[8] There were endurance kissing competitions, marathon hand-holding contests, and milk-drinking, egg-eating, and gum-chewing races. One of the most famous record setters of the 1920s was flagpole sitter Shipwreck Kelly. He emerged on the scene in 1924, shortly after the first wave of dance marathons, but claimed to have had the idea much earlier. Kelly said he had been to see a Jack Dempsey fight down south in 1920 and "there was a bunch of foreigners there, foolin' around. They got playful and threw me out of a third-story window. I hit a flagpole and hung on. That got me started."[9] When reminded that Dempsey didn't fight in 1920, Kelly remembered that the incident had actually taken place in 1921 in New Jersey. Another time he said it had happened in 1922 in Florida and that Dempsey had chased him up a flagpole.[10] Whatever the details, the through line in Kelly's stories is Jack Dempsey. It was as if Kelly wanted to say, "I know the champ, and the champ knows me." He must have thought that the magic and machismo of the Manassa Mauler's reputation would cast a glow on his own lofty pursuits. Fame was something people could catch by association.

Kelly did become famous in his own right. He had a penchant for danger combined with a contempt for superstition that made for singular accomplishments. In 1927 he sat for seven days, thirteen hours, and thirteen minutes on a flagpole atop a thirteen-story building in St. Louis.[11] Standing on a six- to eight-inch disk as his platform, with stirrups attached to the pole to protect him should he fall, Kelly drank coffee, shaved, and had manicures on his perch. By 1928 his fee was $100 a day plus receipts from rooftop admissions. Soon, however, his records were challenged by a host of competitors wanting to capitalize on his notoriety. As time wore on, Kelly sat on fewer flagpoles. He eventually returned to Hell's Kitchen on New York's West Side where he spent the rest of his days. On a cold October day in 1952 he was found by police dead in the street, his pockets full of yellowing newspaper clippings crying out his one-time fame.[12] Kelly's fall from brief and trivial glory left him a man alone, echoing his real beginnings as an orphan whose father was killed in a rigging accident before he was born and whose mother died in childbirth.

In benevolent moments, authorities found Kelly and others like him emblematic of the patriotic spirit of America's founders. Feats of endurance were yet another kind of frontier where Americans could display their ability to prevail. When Avon O. Foreman, a fifteen-year-old Baltimore girl, in emulation of Shipwreck Kelly, sat on an ironing board mounted on a pole in her back yard for ten days, ten hours, ten minutes, and ten seconds, the mayor presented her with an embossed testimonial that praised the teenager for exemplifying "the pioneer spirit of early America."[13] After the mayor's dramatic display of confidence, young people in Baltimore became so enthusiastic about flagpole sitting that the police had to check all the city's flagpoles to make sure they were safe for human occupancy.

Beyond these local stunts were record-breaking achievements that were cause for international as well as national celebration. Aviators Charles A. Lindbergh and Amelia Earhart, and swimmer Gertrude Ederle, in particular, earned enduring celebrity for the records they set. Although Lindbergh, Earhart, and Ederle shared with marathon dancers, flagpole sitters, and other contestants the goal of setting world records, they were categorically different. The aviators and swimmer had special skills and training as well as the means to accomplish their endeavors in the light of international attention. Marathon dancers had no special training; their requisite skill was intemperate stamina and enthusiasm. Although a few of the winners of dance marathons were dance teachers, in these contests the quality of the dancing was never a criterion. More important, American urban record setters had very different purposes and values than their international counterparts. With the adoption of Prohibition in 1921, people opposed to the Eighteenth Amendment increasingly insisted that they be left alone to enjoy themselves in their leisure activities.[14] Marathon dancers supported this sentiment by performing in public their rejection of the puritanical and high-minded seriousness behind Prohibition. The freedom to pursue their dance records was the signature of their American spirit. One did not need to be Lindbergh or Ederle, even an average person could win fame. The dancers' frivolity and stamina were reason enough for their celebrity.

Like Kelly's, Cummings's record was soon challenged. She was quickly surpassed by a series of dancers, most of whom were women. Cummings's world record was first beaten by a student at the University of Strasbourg who danced for thirty-three hours, fifteen minutes, and thirty seconds. The student took six short breaks, totaling eleven minutes and thirty seconds.[15] Within a few days Cummings responded, winning her second and final world title by dancing for fifty hours and two minutes. This record was broken in turn by Helen Mayer, a young salesclerk who worked in the ribbon section of a department store in Cleveland. Mayer established a record of fifty-two hours and sixteen minutes on April 12, 1923. Her victory was accompanied by a statement from a physician, Dr. Charles Walsh, who ignored the winner's badly swollen legs and arms and declared that she could have continued for four or five more hours.[16]

During the first few months of marathon dancing there were no clearly defined methods for operating the contests. Organizers did not charge admission, since dance marathons were not yet considered real spectator entertainment. Dance marathons during this period were homemade happenings with local heros and heroines cheered on by friends and family and a few onlookers. Setting a new nonstop dance record was the chief concern of dancers and fans. At first press accounts of the records set simply stated the amount of time danced. Because the rules had not yet been codified, the earliest records did not state the time taken out to go to the toilet, for example—something that, presumably, every contestant had to do—although occasionally they mentioned that a contestant did not dance for a certain number of minutes during some hours. But these reports did not say whether the minutes "out" were subtracted from the total number of hours danced. Every contest kept track of the dancing in its own way. In the absence of official rules it did not seem to matter. Newspapers kept everyone informed of the tally, creating a kind of consensus about the records. Dancers were mindful of the contingencies of recordkeeping, which they were quick to point out when their own records were under attack. After reading an article that traced marathon dancing back to 1364 in London, suggesting that the current fad was neither new nor unique, dancer Valentina Tuffit retorted that the medieval calendar must have had days that were shorter than at present. Besides, medieval dancing would not have been performed according to modern regulations. And finally, she sniffed, "I don't believe it anyway." [17] This arrogant rejection of history amounted to a dismissal of authority in favor of youth culture.

Civic authorities were displeased by marathon dancing. These officials favored the same kind of puritanical control that Prohibitionists espoused. The first ban on dance marathons was issued on April 10, 1923, in Sunderland, England, where an early record had been set less than two months previously. Many cities on both sides of the Atlantic already had regulations governing the hours and days for public dancing. In Sunderland, for example, the mayor invoked an existing local regulation to uphold a magistrate's decision to ban dancing. Never mind that he had turned a blind eye earlier when those regulations were violated. Regulations against dancing were randomly enforced. In this instance, however, the mayor intended to implement the law. "It is an idiotic idea, verging on lunacy, and the Magistrates will not deviate a hair's breadth from the regular licensed hours." [18] This feeling was shared by many in the United States; however, the social climate would not readily tolerate censorship of this kind.

"Dancing Marathons Whirl in 3 Cities," a front-page headline in the *New York Times* announced on April 15, 1923. The article that followed was the first to explicitly expose the tension between "church people" and advocates of free expression. An incident had taken place in Houston at McMillan's Dancing Academy when the assistant district attorney served warrants on seven contestants charging vagrancy. The summonses were the result of efforts of church members and ministers to stop the dancing. The threat to the dancers aroused a strong reaction in the crowd. Spontaneously, a hundred male spectators stepped forward to defend the dancers. Clearly, they identified with the contestants. For a brief time they came between the authorities and the dancers. What right did the authorities have to interfere with their entertainment? The spectators did not back off until the police decided not to make any arrests and the contest was permitted to continue. The only concession was that the dancers were technically in custody. Mr. McMillan, proprietor of the academy and promoter of the contest, promised to post bond for the dancers. He also decided to make the contest a private party on Sunday, thus avoiding prosecution for violation of the blue laws that regulated work, commerce, and amusements on the Sabbath.[19]

McMillan was clearly a shrewd businessman. He was the first dance hall proprietor to charge spectators a dollar at night and a quarter during the day to watch the seven solo dancers with alternating partners try to break the record set by Helen Mayer. He encouraged the dancers to entertain the crowd in any way they could. One of the dancers, Oscar Strickland, lathered his face and shaved, using a mirror held by his partner while one-stepping around the hall.[20] McMillan also had a flair for spectacle. When Magdaline Williams won the Houston marathon with sixty-five and a half hours of nonstop dancing on April 15, McMillan had her whisked away movie-star style in a limousine to a Turkish bath. Hundreds of onlookers wished her well. At a separate dance party, McMillan awarded Williams a cash prize and a trip to New York. Her victory marked the first report of prize money—fifty dollars—underscoring the money-making potential of marathons for both promoters and dancers.[21] No doubt, contestants, sponsors, and spectators were all interested in the money involved in the contests. Writing about a contest in Cleveland, a journalist commented that the "purse" received by Helen Mayer when she set her record probably helped silence mothers who would otherwise object to the craze.[22]

While the Houston contest was in progress, eight couples and six solo dancers set a new record of fifty-three hours in Baltimore on April 14. The dance stopped only when police ended the "performance" at 1 a.m. on the third day. During the contest dancer Myrtle Smith became engaged to her partner, Samuel Glasner—publicly staging her love. Another woman was accused of dancing her partner, Fred Conrad, into "aberration." After forty-two hours of dancing, Conrad climbed a ladder on the orchestra stage and declined to come down. Eventually, after some prodding, Conrad was helped down and placed under the care of a doctor.[23]

In Cleveland, the third city in whirl, four couples dancing the foxtrot were also trying to break Helen Mayer's record, set in that city on April 12. The most outspoken of the dancers was Russel Brady, a redhaired Irishman who claimed he would out-dance any woman in the world—Cleveland women in particular. His aim was to raise the record to sixty hours. Brady fell short of his own sixty-hour goal when he collapsed after dancing forty-three hours and thirty-eight minutes. Even worse, from his point of view, Madeline Gottschick, a Cleveland woman, put him to shame by dancing sixty-six hours, setting the new world's record on April 16.[24]

This phase of nonstop dance established the basis for future dance marathons. At first individuals, either as couples or solo, competed against a set record. This display developed into several dancers in the same dance hall competing both against one another and against previously established records. With several contestants competing in the same room, a drama of rivals developed. Spectators rooted for their friends and favorites. At first the dancers were lively, but as the hours wore on they drooped, becoming slow and lethargic, barely shuffling their feet. Thus "dance" really came to mean perpetual motion. Rules had to be developed to clarify the terms of the competition. When dancing with a partner, contestants were required to keep their bodies in "dance position." This meant that a contestant's arms had to be around the partner, in the position for dancing, or in something akin to a dance position.

Spectators at dance marathons were interested not only in who would win but also in who could last longer, men or women. Cummings and the other female marathon dancers were not flappers or feminists, but their performances registered a shift in female expression. They could and did outdo men in a specific physical activity. During World War I, to fill labor shortages, women made grenades, ran elevators, collected streetcar fares—jobs women had never done before.[25] After the war, women were well established in public life and felt ready for all sorts of new adventures. However, when the men returned from war, they took back their jobs, so women were forced to use leisure activities as the arena in which to make their mark. Of course, some women continued to work for wages, but the jobs now available to them were routine slots traditionally reserved for women. Blocked out of challenging employment, women made leisure activity the the focus of their energy. This way they did not lose everything they had earned by going to work during the war.

Dance marathons were one stage where this revision of gender roles was played out. Of the record holders, Alma Cummings was a dance teacher, Helen Mayer a department store saleswoman, Magdalene Williams a beauty contest winner, Vera Sheppard a file clerk, and June Curry a waitress. Despite their competition with one another, what they understood collectively was that leisure was the realm where they could make claims, seek autonomy, and win victories, even if for only a few hours. In dance marathons at least, these women rejected their dependency on men. They kept going despite the limits of their male partners, and some people applauded them for doing so.

As early as 1910 urban dancing was seen as the emblem of changing values and ways of life. American men and women gathered in public venues to move their bodies to the new rhythms emerging from black culture. In New York City cabarets installed dance floors so that patrons could try for themselves steps that only exhibition dancers previously performed.[26] Bands played late into the night. Couples crowded the dance floors between the courses of their late-night dinners. In middle- and upper-class night clubs, boundaries between observers, participants, and celebrities were often fluid. Irene and Vernon Castle, among the first stars of the supper clubs and cabarets, slipped from their table onto the dance floor, where spotlights followed their movements. When they had finished, the dance floor filled with enthusiastic imitators who tried to accomplish in their own way what the Castles had expertly demonstrated.[27]

Working-class youths frequented their own neighborhood halls, ballrooms, and saloons equipped with dance floors. After work stenographers, clerks, secretaries, salesgirls, soda jerks, domestic servants, shop girls, factory workers, waitresses, and dance teachers gathered in familiar surroundings to try to become the next marathon dance champion of the world. Dance marathons were a way for them to position themselves, at least momentarily, at center stage. They could earn the transitory fame that was so much a feature of the Roaring Twenties—the decade of the "non-stop flight, the million-dollar gate, the moving picture queen, the new Ford, the White House Spokesman, and the English Channel."[28]

Working-class dance halls had been changing since the beginning of the century. Early twentieth-century dance halls were the outgrowth of the turn-of-the-century "racket" or "affair," established in working-class neighborhoods. These events were sponsored by local organizations. Attendance was a matter of community support as well as sociability. Gradually leisure became increasingly commercialized, and "pleasure" clubs began to sponsor dances that took place alongside the more traditional affairs. As American historian Kathy Peiss points out, these pleasure clubs, catering mostly to young people and run solely for recreation and personal profit, rejected older working-class values that linked recreation, economic service, and intergenerational sociability.[29]

Slowly, commercial venues in zones separated from neighborhood settings began to take over and develop the business of dancing. The Grand Central, New York City's first elaborate twentieth-century "dance palace," was built in 1911. Others, with capacities ranging from five hundred to three thousand, soon followed. But even though these new dance palaces were located in commercial zones, community patronage of the dance event was still deemed important.[30] It gave the semblance of respectability and reassured members of the community of their success in containing the "dangerous" side of dance events. Without community patronage, there was the danger of losing youth to what dance stood for—unmonitored heterosexual contact. In response to this concern, managers of dance halls created their own social clubs. This made it seem that the dances that took place at these new venues were sponsored by clubs or community organizations and were not solely for profit.[31] The managers, proprietors, and promoters thus exploited the notion of organizational sponsorship that was the hallmark of the older neighborhood dance halls, while actually running commercial enterprises for personal gain. In this way they were able to conflate traditional values with free enterprise. They also validated the independence, both personal and economic, of leisure entertainments.

Dance hall proprietors championed youth culture. When warrants were served to dancers in the 1923 marathon contest in Houston, it was McMillan, the promoter of the contest and proprietor of the academy, who stepped in to post the bond for the contestants. McMillan was the host, promoter, proprietor, protector, sponsor, and advocate of both the dance marathon event and the individual dancers. In their roles as both proprietors and protectors, men like McMillan commanded a new kind of respect and notoriety. They engaged in free enterprise while the dancers declared their freedom to engage in the recreation of their choice. Both parental and civic authorities threatened this liberty. When police tried to enforce restrictions on dance marathons, contestants and spectators resisted their authority. They created a drama out of their resistance and cast police and "church ladies" in major roles.

Upper-class, middle-class, and working-class dance venues provided separate settings for their different clienteles, but everyone performed the same dances. Dancers at all these clubs were doing the turkey trot, Texas tommy, bunny hug, foxtrot, and tango. These "hot" dances had an increasingly liberating effect on dancers and spectators alike. Prescribed steps and etiquette left over from the Victorian age were abandoned in favor of dances that encouraged improvisation, syncopated body rhythms, self-expression, and a "close hold." Partners were no longer signed up before the dancing began. Instead, dancers freely chose one another, engaging in a whirl of physical intimacy that was balanced with "break-aways" when partners were free to express their own ideas of bodily synchrony by hunching their torsos and throwing their limbs. Alma Cummings and other marathon dancers danced these dances. Their reliance on multiple partners and choice of dance as an expressive medium indicate that they were very familiar with the new style of public heterosexual behavior.

In their brief history, dance marathons were involved with youth culture, sexuality, gender, entertainment, dancing, and the commercialization of leisure. They were a heated center of debate, a debate jointly fostered by shortsighted proprietors and promoters looking for publicity and concerned citizens looking for ways to restrain "immoral" forces. Dance marathons were quickly identified as a social problem—but this identification helped sell tickets.

In addition to blue laws, specific antimarathon regulations already existed. These laws were originally enacted to prevent the grueling bicycle races that were a fad around the turn of the century. The New York penal code (Section 832, Article 78) read as follows: "In a bicycle race or other contest of skill, speed or endurance, wherein one or more persons shall be contestant or contestants, it shall be unlawful for any contestant to continue in such a race or contest for a longer time than twelve hours during any twenty-four hours. The proprietor, occupant or lessee of the place where such race or contest takes place, consenting to, allowing or permitting any violation of the foregoing provisions of this setting is guilty of a misdemeanor." [32]

Some dancers were willing to go to great lengths to prevent such laws from interfering with their efforts. Two months after Cummings had set her world's record, marathon dancers in the same Audubon ballroom danced out the door and into a waiting van. "Five young men and three girls who had been dancing twenty-eight hours and fifty minutes in New York at midnight last night carried out at that hour an audacious enterprise in order that the police, armed with a meddlesome old law, might not thwart their intention to set a terpsichorean marathon record that should stand for a long time." [33] While they continued to dance, the van transported them to the Edgewater Ferry, where they danced on deck across the Hudson River to New Jersey. When they had arrived at the far shore, the van transported them to the Pekin dance hall in Fort Lee. The dancers chose this alternative when George Grundy, the proprietor of the Audubon ballroom, was issued a summons to appear before a magistrate in Washington Heights court. The court would decide whether the regulation that prohibited marathon contests on Sundays was being violated. Facing criminal charges, Grundy decided to stop the dance marathon at midnight. After the incident in Houston, the police sergeant knew better than to try to stop the dancers. He nodded at them as they danced all around him and smiled at the mothers and fathers and friends who were cheering them on. But when Grundy announced his decision to stop the marathon and close the ballroom, the friendly smiles of the dancers and spectators turned to wailing complaints. It was then that they called the Pekin dance hall to see if it would stay open to receive the marathon dancers. [34]

The press, wholeheartedly on the side of the "brave and daring" contestants, characterized the sergeant who served the summons as a "mean old thing," oblivious to the aspirations of youth alive with civic pride. The dancers were only trying to prove that "right here in New

York there could be dancing longer winded than that about which yesterday's newspapers disclosed Houston, Texas was all excited." [35] Soon after they arrived at the Pekin dance hall in Fort Lee, they discovered they had to leave there too. Their plight was the doing of Sergeant Harnett, an aid to Mayor George Hill of Fort Lee. With references to the New Jersey State Board of Health regulations, as well as to "immoral representations," Sergeant Harnett gave the dancers a 1 a.m. deadline to find yet another place to dance. Convinced that the long arm of the law was predictable enough, the dancers decided to dance no more than twelve hours in any state. They briefly returned to New York, where they continued dancing in a flat in Harlem; only reporters, who were required to keep the address secret, and a few others were admitted to watch. The stint in Harlem was noted for its economy of motion due to limited space and tired legs. The next destination for the interstate dancers was the Cygnet Athletic Club in East Port Chester, Connecticut. The only dancers left by that time were Vera Sheppard and Ben Solar, a couple, and Ted Gill, Henry Howard, and Robert Conklin. In transit, however, due to the bumping and rattling of the van, the dancers were creating steps that would alarm any dancing master. They were "tripping a toe that if not light was at least fantastic." [36] When the van arrived at the Cygnet Club at 2:10 a.m., only Ben Solar and Vera Sheppard were still dancing; the other three had fallen asleep.

At 8:20 a.m. Solar suddenly began to wander aimlessly. After being revived with smelling salts and cold water, he was led back to Sheppard. He made a determined effort to resume dancing but collapsed after a few minutes and was disqualified. He had been dancing for more than two days. Sheppard continued with various relief partners. By that afternoon, attempts at rhythm and formal dance steps had been abandoned. The "dancing" had become a painful ambling walk performed in a dreary slow motion. Shortly after 2:30 p.m. the police arrived with word that the contest had to stop. In the end, they consented to let it run until the new record of sixty-nine hours was set on April 17. [37]

Vera Sheppard broke Madeline Gottschick's Cleveland record of sixty-six hours and six minutes and reached her sixty-nine-hour goal at 4:10 p.m. She was carried off the dance floor in the arms of cheering friends. Sheppard had been dancing from Friday evening until Monday afternoon. The evening of her victory she appeared at the Audubon Ballroom in New York for a celebration in her honor. In answer to reporters' questions of "how she did it," friends told how she did not smoke and was very abstemious in what she ate and drank. Her sister claimed that Vera prayed every night. Impatient with these explanations, the heroine herself decisively claimed, "I'm Irish; do you suppose I could have stuck it out otherwise?"[38] Asked about the time she spent dancing, Sheppard reported, "While I was dancing I never thought of being tired. I kept thinking what good fun it was. The only thing that annoyed me was having a man's arm around me all the time."[39] At the celebration Sheppard consented to a few dances with admirers and then was reunited with Ben Solar; together they were heralded as "the championship long-distance dance team of the world." The atmosphere at the celebration was familiar to Sheppard because after her eight-to-five job as a file clerk in a large office on Long Island, she used to travel to the Audubon Ballroom in Manhattan to teach dance until midnight.[40] But this night was a night unlike any other, marked as it was with her fleeting celebrity.

After Sheppard's well-publicized, successful evasion of blue laws and her marathon victory, contestants were expected to cleverly evade any authority that tried to disrupt their efforts to break a record. Contestants were portrayed by sympathetic reporters as being at the mercy of all forms of authority, from doctors who advised them to stop dancing to floor judges who made sure they kept moving. Thus there were two structures of control: civic and medical authority, and the authority of floor judges and promoters. The press was always there to report any confrontation. As dance marathons developed, this clash between contestants and those who wanted to control them was incorporated into the drama of the event itself.

As the "official" recorder of dance marathons, the press was also a form of authority that legitimized records and sanctioned winners. When Madeline Gottschick was informed that her record had been surpassed by Sheppard, she refused to concede the championship. She reasoned that "much of their dancing was done in moving vans without witnesses and I question whether it is an official record."[41] Gottschick's protests fell on deaf ears largely because the reporters had already made up their minds.

By April 19, 1923, both Gottschick and Sheppard had been undone by challengers in Cleveland. By press time on that day, Arthur Howard Klein had been dancing for eighty-two hours and was still going strong. He had wiped out a record of seventy-three hours set earlier in the day by Magdaline Wolfe, the first person to break Sheppard's record. Upon learning that her record had been broken, Sheppard challenged the new champion to a match. She would need two weeks to get her feet back in condition, she said. Grundy offered to sponsor the event in any state where the contest would be legal and suggested that the event be witnessed by a committee of judges to ensure fair play.[42] There is no record of the event ever happening.

By the middle of April marathon dancing already had a long list of proponents and detractors. Spectators were willing to pay to watch young men and women dance the foxtrot and one-step for hours on end to jazz music played by an orchestra or phonograph. Promoters had begun thinking about what might make the spectacle more entertaining. Those opposed to dance marathons asserted they were demoralizing and dangerous. "There is nothing inspiring in seeing an extremely tired pretty girl in a worn bathrobe, dingy white stockings in rolls about scuffling slippers, her eyes half shut, her arms hung over her partner's shoulders, drag aching feet that seemed glued to the floor in one short, agonizing step after another."[43] Louis H. Chalif, vice president of the American Society of Teachers of Dancing, asserted that the contests were "dangerous to health, useless as entertainment and a disgrace to the art and profession of dancing."[44] Evelyn Hubbell, official judge of dancing at the Terrace Garden Dance Palace, corroborated this opinion when she told the press that it was physically impossible to continue any dance style more than twenty hours before the steps became blurred beyond recognition.[45] Some people thought the dancing was immoral. In the factory town of Cedar Grove, Louisiana, a hundred and fifty men and women left a combined Methodist-Presbyterian church meeting to crash a marathon dance. They succeeded in forcing the dancers to leave town.[46]

To Mina Van Winkle, chief of the Woman's Bureau of the Washington, D.C., Police Department, the situation seemed like an epidemic, but she could not imagine how to contain it. Concerning one planned marathon, she said, "I have received calls all day from prominent citizens and social workers, asking me to forbid the affair, but I can't." More ominously, Chief Van Winkle predicted that the dancing epidemic was a sure sign of war. "A dance epidemic always precedes national disaster, as clouds precede a storm," she cautioned. "A prominent historian tells us that dance fevers always come before revolution. America is dancing herself to war."[47] Dr. Arthur P. Noyes, chief executive officer of a federal institution for the insane, also warned of potential for devastation following marathon dancing: "A similar plague hit England in 1364. People danced around for three or four days, until they fell in the streets. The present craze is fast growing into the epidemic stage; it is not a disease but a mania that is manifest in the religious sect of Holy Rollers." Fears such as these promoted the first ban on dance marathons in the United States. When imposing the ban in the middle of April, Mayor Curley of Boston flatly declared, "It is foolishness to try to establish long distance terpsichorean records."[48]

"Objective" theories were used to try to understand dance marathons. Dr. Danby Tewfuit, identified as a noted Freudian psychologist and a philosopher, saw as either "Uniquitists" or "Giganticists" all long-distance or nonstop walkers, dancers, piano players, poetry reciters, roller skaters, building climbers, perambulator pushers, and pie, oyster, watermelon, or cake eaters, as well as the Niagara Falls barrel artists. Uniquitists, victims of a "uniquity complex," yearned to do something no one else had ever done. Giganticists, victims of a "giganticist complex," wanted to do something—anything—more times than anyone else. "A characteristic of practically all such people," said Dr. Tewfuit, "is their utter regardlessness of the medium of obtaining their extraordinary desires. Sometimes the two complexes overlap, and occasionally substitute for each other."[49] While no one was certain about the precise meaning of Dr. Tewfuit's explanation, it did serve as something to consider when all other interpretations failed.

Equally important to many of those who opposed nonstop dancing was a concern for health. It could not possibly be good for a person to dance for so long. Doctors were soon predicting permanent damage to the nervous system and muscles. Assistant Surgeon General M. J. White issued this graphic public statement: "It's the same as putting a five-ton load on a one-ton truck. Something must give. No nervous system, no matter how strong, can stand seventy hours of dancing without ill-effects. It may result in overstrained heart, rupture the muscles or cause serious injury to the nerves of the body. The dancers may not notice it for months but the strain they put their bodies is certain to tell."[50] Several dance marathons required contestants to pass physical exams before competing. When Chicago health commissioner Herman Bundesen learned about police interference with dance marathons in other cities on the grounds that they jeopardized health, he felt pressed to make a statement. While acknowledging that he believed three hours was the limit of healthful dancing, Commissioner Bundesen reassured the public that he would not stop dance marathons: "Chicago health authorities will not interfere with any one who wishes to dance himself to death."[51] Unfortunately for some, this glib remark did not exaggerate the possible consequences of nonstop dancing. On April 14, twenty-seven-year-old Homer Morehouse of North Tonawanda, New York, dropped dead from heart failure as he left the dance floor with his partner after dancing eighty-seven hours on a wager. His was the first reported death to result from marathon dancing.[52]

By April 17 physicians in Philadelphia had declared that the contests caused dilation of the heart and were generally detrimental to health. In the opinion of Dr. Wilmer Krusen, Dr. Arthur M. Dannenberg, and Dr. William A. Stecher, marathon dancing was exceedingly dangerous and without any possible benefit.[53]

While many mayors and health authorities, following Surgeon General White's warning, were trying to ban dance marathons in their cities, many managers, proprietors, and promoters were opening the contests in established dance halls. By June 1923 contests had taken place in Cleveland, Baltimore, New York, Houston, San Antonio, Boston, Philadelphia, Buffalo, Flint, Norfolk, Dallas, Washington, Youngstown, St. Louis, and Chicago.[54] The effort to keep marathon dancing alive was both anti-authoritarian and nationalistic. An enthusiastic reporter explained: "The good, old-fashioned, 100 percent American who thrills afresh at each new demonstration of the superiority of his homeland over other nations of the earth may just as well go up in the attic and get out the flags and dust them off and get ready to celebrate. . . . For it is in the field of dancing that Yankee grit is scoring another triumph. Barring the interference of the law—and what are laws when they go counter both to personal liberty and international rivalry?—right here in our own country will be established—may already have been established—a record for nonstop dancing that may endure for eternity."[55]

Many of the record setters won their small portion of eternity when the *Literary Digest* published the following list of winners on May 5, 1923:

March 6	Sunderland, England, 9:30
March 6	Edinburgh, 14:39
March 20	Marseilles, France, 24:04

March 31   New York, Miss Alma Cummings, 27:00
April 6   New York, Miss Ruth Molleck and Jack Butler, 40:00
April 9   New York, Miss Alma Cummings, 50:00
April 12   Cleveland, Miss Helen Mayer, 52:16
April 14   Baltimore, 53:00 (eight couples and six others stopped by police)
April 15   Houston, Miss Magdalene Williams, 65:53
April 16   Cleveland, Miss Madeline Gottschick, 66:00
April 17   New York, Miss Vera Sheppard, 69:00
April 19   Cleveland, Arthur Klein, 88:18
April 19   Cleveland, Miss June Curry, 90:10[56]

In the reports of dance marathons from February to June 1923, the rules governing the rest periods taken by the dancers gradually evolved. Clear-cut rules made records consistent with a unified set of standards, and they also provided a neat sidestep when authorities wished to enforce the twelve-hour limit. If dancers took a rest break, they were technically no longer dancing nonstop. The first mention of formal rest periods was in connection with a World War I veteran, R. J. Newman of Dallas. "Friends and admirers put him through a vigorous massage treatment at rest periods and he goes back on the floor at the sound of the gong like the prize fighter."[57] His rest periods were fifteen minutes every four hours.

The development of rest periods may have been the bright idea of a manager or promoter who was looking for a way to enhance the drama of the dance marathons. "The Texas contender [R. J. Newman] at times appears to be in a mental daze, shuffling about with his eyes half closed in an aimless sort of way, while at others he accepts a dancing partner and skims over the floor like a fresh dancer."[58] With rest periods, contestants were no longer simply dragging until they stopped altogether. Their energy ebbed and flowed in dramatic cadences that developed into a performance rhythm. Beyond that, of course, contestants could keep going much longer if they took short periods of rest. Longer contests meant a bigger take at the door. On May 9 R. J. Newman set the record at 160 hours and 55 minutes—almost seven days. He stopped dancing on the advice of physicians.[59]

Newman held the world's record longer than most contestants. It was not until May 27 that his record was broken by Frances Mayer and

Harry Wagner of Youngstown, Ohio, a couple who "in continuous performance" completed 182 hours and 8 minutes of dancing at the East Youngstown Pavilion. Mayer and Wagner rested three minutes every eight hours.[60]

The dance marathon contests in the spring of 1923 were the nascent version of what soon became a new form of popular entertainment. The first flurry of records was reported nationally many times in lengthy front-page stories from February to June. The *New York Times* announced the last record setter of this phase of marathon dancing. In St. Louis on June 10, 1923, Bernie Brand, the sole survivor of a contest that had begun with twenty-two couples, set the record for nonstop dance at 217 hours. He won five thousand dollars in prizes.[61] Dance marathons soon became a feature attraction at local dance halls, receiving publicity mostly from the local press. The first phase of the national furor was over.

Two

THE DANCE DERBY OF THE CENTURY

How great a debt we owe to the press, which frequently
makes the record of life more entertaining than life itself.

Nation, 23 June 1928

Whether or not dance marathons were boring or exciting entertainment, their promoters definitely engaged the press in a manner that made them controversial. Promoter and publicist Milton Crandall was a mastermind of designing spectacles for reporters to write about. He was an important link in the transition of dance marathons from hourly contests to entertainment spectacles. In 1928 Crandall's "Dance Derby of the Century" held at Madison Square Garden in New York was paradigmatic of what dance marathons were to become. Crandall had the idea of amplifying the interactions between contestants and interspersing them with special attractions. His innovations were based on the recognition that such events challenge not only the strength of the dancers but also the endurance of the audience. From the promoter's point of view, the question was how to make the marathon last long enough to make money. The marathon's duration is finally determined by the audience, not the dancers, because the event is over—at least financially—when the audience loses interest. This could happen before the dancers ran out of steam. So there were really two tests of endurance going on, and they were linked in fascinating ways.

As a skilled promoter Crandall knew that the performance of endurance alone could not hold the audience's attention. He invented several strategies to keep the audience interested in the event. One of the cleverest was the overlap between contest and theater. Marathons were events with delayed outcomes, but whose process was continuous and uneventful. Producing them as theater was Crandall's solution to the problem of audience interest in what was otherwise a long and repetitious contest.

Between 1923 and 1928 dance marathons grew from simple hourly contests to entertainment spectacles lasting several days and sometimes weeks. The spectacles parodied and elaborated on early dance marathons. They emphasized the narrative that tended to emerge while couples were dancing for days at a time. They also self-consciously imitated for comic and melodramatic effect the display of suffering that characterized the earlier marathons. This addition of the simulation of a dance marathon to the actual marathon was central to their popular and commercial success. The development of rules determining hourly periods of rest, along with the added theatricality enabled dance marathons to last for profitable weeks and months. Although the initial 1923 hourly dance records clearly served as a point of departure for the later dance marathons, there is virtually no information on how the metamorphosis happened. The former contestants and promoters I interviewed claimed that the 1923 contests were the predecessors to later dance marathons, but there is almost no written record. In any case, Crandall's 1928 "Dance Derby of the Century" was exemplary of the changes that were taking place.

Spectators became as concerned with the ongoing interactions of the contestants—the "narrative" of the event—as they were with the outcome of the contest. Consequently, several themes began to be associated with dance marathons: covert longings for power and revenge; the comedy and melodrama of ill-suited couples; male culprits responsible for the suffering of women; the reformation of the rake; even marriages between contestants. These themes and the personalities that they evolved were largely familiar to the public. They were drawn from popular novels, live theatrical entertainment, and film.[1] As promoters and contestants alike became increasingly self-conscious about the dramatization of dance marathons, they became more skilled at theatricalizing the themes that were associated with them.

Marathons before Crandall's had mixed entertainment and contest, but none was so famous or so financially successful. Crandall's marathon at Madison Square Garden was the first to fully exploit the duplicitous notions of reality that emerged between the world wars. Crandall's marathon featured a disjunction between the actual contest and its dramatization, and therefore between what was performed and how it was received. This performative disjunction was part of a larger cultural pattern that emerged before the turn of the century. Numerous technical inventions had created the possibility of exploiting the dissociation between an action and its reception. The telephone and phonograph served as means of communication, but they were also vehicles for disembodied sound. Photography and film severed images from their contexts. Dance marathons followed suit by creating fiction from real life (the contest) and real life from fiction (the dramatization of the contest). Advertising had already exploited the conflation of the fictional with the real. "We grew up founding our dreams on the infinite promises of American advertising," Zelda Fitzgerald recalled. By buying the product, advertisers proposed, one could acquire the promise of the image. Never mind that this was and still is magical thinking. No one seemed to care that advertising and films were fiction. The claim of both genres to represent some form of daily life caused viewers to act out their fictional proposals. Everyone became a performer. Personality, the successful performance of self, replaced character as the most desirable American attribute. For Americans who avidly partook of mass and popular culture, daily life was lived between the quotation marks of performance, "as if for real."

By 1928 dance marathons lasting at least a week were taking place in many cities around the country, including Minneapolis, Detroit, Atlantic City, and Pittsburgh. In New York City they took place in downtown Manhattan and in uptown Harlem. The presentation and management of the marathons became less haphazard than before as promoters and publicity agents took over and professionalized the events. As a result, dance marathons became a commodity in the live entertainment industry. Because individual promoters insisted on formulating their own shows, they could not agree upon rules and procedures. The length of time contestants were to dance, acceptable behavior on the dance floor, and rules for elimination all varied from one marathon to the next. Although this lack of standardized rules was troublesome, it allowed the marathons to easily absorb a variety of influences from other forms of popular entertainment.

Crandall's career demonstrates the fluid boundaries that existed in the 1920s between different forms of popular entertainment. According to Paul Sann in *Fads, Follies and Delusions of the American People,* Crandall's first theatrical venture was touring with a panorama of the Dayton flood. Next he went to Hollywood where he collected a group of aging movie stars whom he booked for one-night stands in the small towns he had come to know while touring with the panorama. Crandall followed his Hollywood venture with a road tour of motion pictures. In 1927 he opened a ballroom in Pittsburgh.[2] Although Sann does not cite sources for his account of Crandall's endeavors, the stories probably were part of the mystique and myth of a promoter noted for creating an aura around his activities. Crandall's experiences served him well as a dance marathon promoter. He was able to combine narratives and performance structures from several different genres of popular entertainment. His "Dance Derby of the Century" created an ambiance drawn from horse shows, roof gardens, and ballrooms, placed in the service of a performance that was part dance contest, part vaudeville, and part exhibition dance.

Crandall himself was pudgy and balding, with an air that managed to be simultaneously innocent and yet somehow sinister. His persona helped attract the public attention he needed to promote his ventures, and reporters tended to focus on it in their stories. Every article that discussed the Madison Square Garden show featured Crandall in some way. His announcements at the marathon, his profits, his plans for a show in Europe (which never happened), and his comments about the contestants were all deemed as newsworthy as the marathon itself. Crandall was known as having a flair for gimmicks and an ability to crush his opponents. He was "sometimes called professor, sometimes called doc, and sometimes called other things."[3] His reputation as a first-rate publicist was well deserved; it was Crandall who promoted actress Clara Bow as the "It Girl." Everyone knew the unspeakable "It" was sex.

From the beginning of his dance marathon career, Crandall played the roles of both publicist and promoter. Just before staging the Madison Square Garden marathon, Crandall had managed a ballroom in Pittsburgh. There he had talked with some dancers who claimed they could dance all night. After receiving permission from the local board of health and police, he opened a marathon using his own dancers as the nucleus of the show.[4] Sunday blue laws put the event to rest after six days, but it was so successful that Crandall decided to open another one in Homestead, Pennsylvania, with the same contestants. In both cases, he was able to get the Associated Press and the United Press International to take notice. Crandall's ventures in Pittsburgh and Homestead were lucrative, and rumors circulated of enormous profits, perhaps as much as $65,000. In any case, Crandall now felt confident enough to speculate on a much larger show in a much larger city.[5] The Madison Square Garden show was to be cosponsored by Crandall and Tex Rickards, who in 1926 had promoted the Garden's highly successful six-day bicycle race.

According to Jimmy Scott, a ballroom dancer and prize winner in the 1928 marathon, newspapers gave greater coverage to the "Dance Derby of the Century" than to any previous entertainment attraction in memory. "Reporters and photographers were assigned daily running stories; trade papers and magazines ran special articles; for columnists it was a bonanza! . . . One tabloid [the New York *Evening Graphic*], claiming to be opposed to continuing The Derby, ran retouched photos and exaggerated stories with a horror angle, which, no doubt, created longer lines at the box office."[6]

Publicity was a crucial factor in turning the Garden marathon into the entertainment event of the year. Crandall knew how to solicit the publicity needed to attract a large audience. Provoking scandal and notoriety were among the best methods of attracting attention, especially on the part of the tabloids. Tabloid newspapers, modeled on London counterparts, had come to the United States with the founding of the *New York Daily News* in 1919. The *Daily News* was an immediate success, and after five years it had the largest circulation of any paper in New York. William Randolph Hearst followed with the *Daily Mirror*, and Bernarr MacFadden jumped in with the *New York Evening Graphic*. These papers, which collectively had millions of readers, gave Crandall daily visibility to a mass of potential spectators. Clearly, the savvy

Crandall decided to capitalize on the possibilities offered by the tab-loids' penchant for dramatizing the mundane. He emphasized for the press the daily "domestic" narratives that included contestants having manicures and foot treatments—and quarrels. The tabloid accounts of these occurrences took the tone of sensational testimonial. "Oblivion Eases Torture" was the *Evening Graphic* caption for a photograph of Vera Campbell receiving a manicure and having her hair done while sleeping.[7]

Crandall cleverly billed his show as the "Dance Derby of the Cen-tury." Contestants were competing for the "International Endurance Dancing Championship" and a $5,000 prize. In devising such a title for the event Crandall recalled all previous dance marathons and pointed to the primacy of his own show. The press reported it as a spectacle featuring outrageous personalities, sadistic and masochistic couples, championship dancers, and just plain ordinary people. The *Evening Graphic* published incendiary headlines throughout the marathon: "2 More Crack under Mad Dance," "Gamblers Clean Up at Dance Mara-thon," "Nine Couples Alive after 394th Hour." What more could an audience demand?

On June 10, 1928, everything was ready to go. The press was buzzing, the contestants were waiting, and New Yorkers were curious about this newest attempt to break the world record for continuous dancing. After commending the dancers and Crandall for their "American spirit," Andrew J. "Bossy" Gillis, listed on the program as the "world's champi-onship endurance mayor," fired three shots, and ninety-one couples began dancing to the strains of "Sweet Sue, I Love You."[8]

The couples were dressed up for an evening on the town. Collectively they were optimistic. They had seen World War I come and go. They had experienced the postwar Depression and recovery. Women had won the right to vote. And while Prohibition was the law of the land, it did not stop men and women from pursuing leisure entertainment, in-cluding drinking. Prosperity seemed to be the destiny of every Ameri-can to whom President Herbert Hoover had promised "a chicken in every pot and two cars in every garage." In roof gardens, speakeasies, and dance palaces all classes of people mingled and toasted the intoxi-cating elixir of freedom of expression. Their frivolity, however, could not erase the consciousness that industrialization coupled the new prosperity with a new peril. Poverty was visible but not spoken about.

Urban Americans were marked with a tension that begged for urgent expression.

Everyone who entered the dance marathon had to sign an agreement releasing the management from responsibility for what might happen to them during the event. The dancers also had to turn over to Crandall's management any theatrical or motion picture engagements that resulted from winning the contest.[9] Crandall was justified in thinking that some contestants might use the contest to procure further entertainment engagements, since the event attracted many participants who had some show business experience.

Before any contestant was accepted, she or he had to pass a medical examination. The doctors and nurses listened to contestants' hearts, took their temperatures, and generally searched for physical defects. Only one man was refused entrance.[10] On June 10, 1928, the *Times* reported that 106 couples had turned up for the exam and latecomers were expected. The next day the *Times* reported that ninety-one couples had started the contest, but by June 12, 132 couples were said to be dancing for the $5,000 prize money.

As Rickards had done for contestants in the six-day bicycle race, Crandall provided red-and-white canvas booths for the participants furnished with chairs and cots, set up around the perimeter of the arena. Larger tents were also installed to house doctors, nurses, referees, and beauticians. During rest periods, dancing couples were expected to retire to their booths to eat, sleep, and receive attention from their private trainers and masseurs or masseuses, whom they paid out of their own pockets. When the interval was over a tugboat whistle summoned contestants back to the dance floor. While the booths afforded the contestants some privacy and the semblance of home, they also signaled just how far the dancers were from their usual domestic lives.

Patriotic bunting, interspersed with advertising banners, was hung around the ceiling at the level of the highest bleachers. Such gestures emphasized the continuation of post–World War I patriotism and also served, in general, to assuage anxiety about the national sympathies of a population with a large number of immigrants. Americanism meant purity both of intention and of ethnic background. "New York," wrote one commentator at the end of the 1920s, "has been a cesspool into which immigrant trash has been dumped for so long that it can scarcely be considered American any more."[11] The "Dance Derby of the Century"

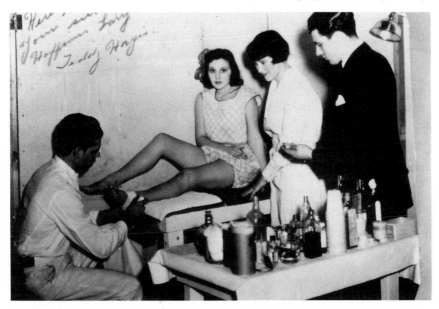

Treating injuries in a marathon "hospital" open to the view of the audience
became a regular feature at dance marathons. (Photo from the Dance Collection
of New York City Public Library, Lincoln Center)

was not immigrant entertainment. It was for those who were already
situated, however poorly, in American life.

Patriotism and purity went well with advertising. Set up around the
perimeter of the Garden were booths of "footease peddlers," shoe merchants, and hosiery vendors ready to serve the dancers.[12] At one end of
the arena was a very large clock with the goal of 140 hours clearly
marked for everyone to see. In fact, Crandall hoped the contest would
run 1,200 hours. One large banner read: "Winners will receive five
thousand dollars and a tour of vaudeville."

Box seats were placed on the dance floor. Patrons who reserved these
seats wore evening clothes—something that, according to dancer Scott,
lent the event the prestige of a horse show.[13] A platform stage was built
in the center of the arena for the orchestra and master of ceremonies.
Around the stage, speakers were installed to amplify the Victrola that
spelled the orchestra during breaks. The potted palms around the stage
and in the center of the floor suggested the kind of stylishness commonly associated with posh roof gardens or ballrooms.

Evening clothes were not the only equestrian allusion. Dance marathons were often called dance "derbies," and printed daily reports issued by the management became known as "dope sheets." Solidly built contestants who could stay through the show with sheer grit and stamina were "horses." The term could also be used derogatorily because, although they were admired for their stamina, marathon "horses" were not known for skilled dancing or first-class entertainment.

The entrants in the "Dance Derby of the Century" included eleven runners who had previously competed in Pyle's Bunion Derby, the first cross-country race from Los Angeles to New York, held in 1928. Other entrants were a channel swimmer, several nonstop-dancing champions, physical culturists, several brother-and-sister teams, and fairly well-known ballroom dancers from the New York area. Marianne Jacque and her partner Edward J. Leonard were among the experienced marathon dancers. Jacque had danced for sixty-one hours and fifty-four minutes in a contest with fifteen-minute rest periods every six hours. Leonard had danced 122 hours, but in a contest with more frequent rest periods.[14]

Tommy Nolan and Ann King, a champion Charleston team from Pittsburgh, entered the contest, as did ballroom dancers Jimmy Scott and Olga Christensen. Before the contest, Scott spent thirty-nine weeks in George White's *Manhattan Mary* at the Apollo Theater. Crandall wanted to be sure that at least some of the contestants were entertainers. He confessed to the press that he was paying some of the professional dance teams an honorarium of $1,000 for participating in the marathon.[15] A dozen couples were registered from foreign countries, the largest number coming from Italy. At sixty-four years of age, long-distance runner C. W. Hart was the oldest entrant.[16] Also entering the contest was Baron Giorgio Mario Suriani of Naples who, some months earlier, had advertised his title for sale in a Boston newspaper for an asking price of $100,000. The baron's retiring booth was decorated with his coat of arms. He and his partner, Señorita Bella Bella Insurtilla of Madrid, were Couple Number 1.[17] Crandall had made sure the "Dance Derby of the Century" was well stocked with interesting personalities and entertainers.

Twenty-seven hours after the contest began, it was reported that ninety-seven couples remained on the dance floor. A great deal was happening. The baron and Señorita Insurtilla were not getting along, and their arguments led the couple to drop out of the contest. After they quit, each accused the other of leaving first. The baron refused to vacate his "royal box" and insisted, as he was still able to dance, that the management find him another partner. At the same time, Señorita Insurtilla maintained that it was the baron who had quit, claiming that for the final two hours of dancing together she had had to carry his weight. The scene ended with the baron gathering up his dinner clothes and dress shirts and leaving the Garden in a huff while threatening lawsuits.[18]

Dramatic vignettes like this one helped to break up the long hours of the contest, and several were usually in progress at the same time. Members of the audience returned day after day to see new developments. It did not matter if the baron and his señorita were "real" or not, because once narratives such as these were introduced, contest and theater overlapped and intermingled. These narratives generated dramatic tension by punctuating the slow hours of the contest with different themes that spun their own emotional webs. Some of the popular narratives at dance marathons concluded in a manner similar to that of the baron and Señorita Insurtilla: there was mounting discord and then a rupture, resulting in the contestants dropping out or being disqualified. Other narratives had no solution or end. They simply stopped without closure or denouement.

On the second day of the marathon, beauty parlor and barber chairs were installed on the arena floor for the contestants. The women contestants flocked to the beauty parlor to have their hair washed and curled and their faces massaged, while the men lined up at the barber chair for a shave. One writer speculated that most of the women had bobbed their hair to avoid carrying extra weight. To save time—everything had to be finished in the allotted fifteen-minute rest period—the men lathered themselves before they sat down in the chair. And since the time was always too short for a beauty parlor session, several women were still receiving manicures after they returned to the dance floor.[19]

Grooming rituals were a calculated part of the spectacle and carefully staged to take place in full view. While demonstrating the extent to which contestants had been pulled away from their daily routines, these little scenes also simulated an aura of domesticity and helped create an illusion of intimacy on the part of the audience. Like other illusions at dance marathons, the contestants created them, but they did not share them.

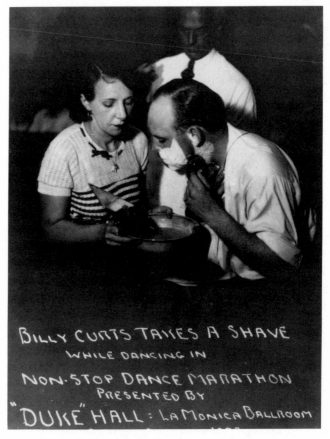

BILLY CURTS TAKES A SHAVE
WHILE DANCING IN
NON-STOP DANCE MARATHON
PRESENTED BY
"DUKE" HALL : La Monica Ballroom

Billy Curts shaving on the dance floor. Displays of private grooming were part
of early dance marathons. (Photo from the collection of Carol Martin)

Contrary to illusion was the actual discomfort and pain of the contestants. The audience at Madison Square Garden enjoyed this as much as any other aspect of the marathon. In a commentary in the *Times*, one writer noted that "it was [historian Thomas] Macaulay's conjecture that the Puritans objected to bear-baiting not because it gave pain to the bear but because it gave pleasure to the spectators. This is a much more tolerant age. Apparently it welcomes marathon dances despite the obvious fact that they give pain to the dancers and leaves one wondering what kind of spectator might derive pleasure from the frowsy spectacle." [20] Although framed as criticism of the marathon and its spectators, commentary like this did as much to build attendance as to discourage it. No doubt there was pain in dancing for days at a time, but by portraying the suffering in a way that drew attention to the event, the press undermined critical distance in service of sensational feature articles that made people want to attend the spectacle.

All the contestants had to follow the rules of the competition or risk elimination. The Crandall show, like others of this period, had its own rules. They read as follows:

Rules

All of the entrants competing have been pronounced physically fit by the Official Medical Board who will be in attendance at all times throughout the contest. Teams may be backed by a City, Chamber of Commerce, Ballroom or business enterprise. Changes of wearing apparel will be allowed during the rest periods only. Contestants who do not keep fully dressed in accordance with the regulation are subject to disqualification. No changes of partners will be permitted. When one member of a team withdraws, the entry is withdrawn. Rules and regulations will be strictly enforced by the referee. Expert masseurs, masseuses, hairdressers, tonsorial artists, manicurists, chiropodists, and other attendants for the comfort of the dancers will be in attendance at all times. Contestants are required to dance one hour and rest fifteen minutes making a total of 60 minutes dancing and 15 minutes rest. The rest period must be taken simultaneously by all dancers desiring to take advantage of the rest period, but teams are permitted to dance on without taking the rest if they so desire; but if the entrants do not take the rest period this does not permit them to add the elapsed time to their new rest period. Waltz, fox-trot, two-step and smile five-minute sprints for cash prizes will be staged throughout the contest. Entrants, however, are not compelled to enter these sprints unless they so wish. The rules do not require entrants to be dancing, as long as they are in the dance position and moving. Should partners separate while on the floor, the floor manager is instructed to give them a ten-minute warning. Failure to then be in position will result in the team being eliminated.[21]

Crandall's rules clearly showed how marathons had changed since 1923. Couples were now an inseparable unit. If one dropped out, the other had to leave too. Concern for contestants' health and grooming had become part of the spectacle of the event. Time was broken into discrete hourly units of rest and dancing. Actual dancing was not required, just continual motion and some semblance of the dance position. "Sprints" were added as an additional spectacle in which contestants could compete for money.

While rules made marathons orderly and profitable, no one suggested at this stage of the entertainment that one set of rules should govern all marathons. Contestants were concerned about the ratio of rest periods and dancing, but they also wanted to be able to make deals with promoters when they could. Ideally, the standardization of rules would circumvent this possibility and would prevent promoters from making the rules more difficult when they wanted to put more pressure on the dancers. In reality it did not work that way. Rules were established at the beginning of every marathon, but they were open for revision by promoters, and generally the promoters did revise them. With the addition of rest periods contestants could dance much longer, so promoters had to find ways to keep marathons interesting for days and weeks at a time. Changing the amount of rest from fifteen minutes to ten or five minutes could help provide the tension needed to sustain a show. In turn, added tension could make possible an increase in ticket prices. Crandall's dance marathon was so successful in this respect that ticket prices went from $1.50 the first night to $3.30 by the second week.[22]

During the course of the show contestants competed for additional cash prizes donated by celebrities, by sponsors of individual couples, and by the audience, all of whom also served as judges of the competition. At first ballroom dancers Jimmy Scott and Olga Christensen decided not to participate in these extra competitions in order to save their energy. But after they realized that an occasional burst of real dancing could revive their spirits, they changed their minds. The first contest they won was literally a mistake. Feeling tired, they decided to dance the next dance full out. "Ramona" was the tune, and Scott and Christensen did a waltz tango. Much to their surprise, after they finished, their trainer told them they had a won a waltz exhibition contest. The partners had not heard the announcement about the special contest because announcements were so frequent that they did not pay any attention to them.[23] Most of the other expert dance teams fell out of the marathon by the fifth day. This left no competitors in the contest who could equal the dancing ability of Scott and Christensen. Their fans started sending them donations, via the master of ceremonies, ranging from five dollars to fifty dollars, with a request for an exhibition dance.

Together they earned $1,300 in special contest prizes and exhibition donations.[24] One source estimated that a total of $10,000 was donated by celebrities and spectators for such special contests and exhibitions at the Garden show.[25]

When the notorious speakeasy owner Texas Guinan showed up at the Garden she was asked to come on stage to say a few words. Guinan's proclivity for publicity was just as sharp as Crandall's. In an evening dress and fur cape she sauntered from her seat to the microphone, waved to the crowd, paused, and then uttered her trademark phrase, "Hello, suckers." The audience cheered and laughed. Guinan made them know that the whole thing was a bit of a con and congratulated them for their willingness to play along. Guinan's own persona embodied the openly illicit nightlife of the 1920s. "Where in the hell would I be without prohibition?" was her response to a raid on one of her clubs.[26] As she did at her speakeasy, Guinan encouraged irreverence and heckling. Before leaving the marathon she commented in the same ironic tone, reminiscent of Mae West: "Compared to Milton Crandall Nero himself was a neophyte. He [Crandall] came over to my club the other night and I told him I believed it was my duty to serve him ground glass. Such unpaid tortures as he instigated hurt my feelings."[27]

Frequently featured in the tabloids during the dry raids of 1927–28, Guinan needed no introduction to the marathon audience. Thanks to the press, everyone knew that all one needed to do for admittance to the series of speakeasies Guinan ran between 1924 and 1930 was to knock twice on a sliding panel set in the door and tell the person who appeared, "Joe sent me."[28] Once inside club customers felt at ease in the atmosphere of bonhomie. Armed with a clapper, which she was fond of using on prominent customers' heads, or a police whistle, Guinan sat on a stool at the center of the main room and directed the tone, movement, and drink of the night. Waiters kept their eyes on her and watched for her nod signaling that a customer who asked for liquor should receive it.[29] Guinan claimed she sold only set-ups for customers who brought their own liquor, not bothering to account for the brisk business she did in Scotch and champagne.[30]

By the sixth day of the dance marathon only twenty-nine couples remained circling the arena. Transcontinental runner William R. Downing dropped out because his partner Florence Lillian Anderson was weak. Mabel Stewart and Joe Schultz were eliminated when Mabel fell asleep during the fifteen-minute rest period and her mother did not have the heart to wake her up. Channel swimmer Wylda Davies and her partner Robert J. Cole, Jr., just decided to go home. An official from the Amateur Athletic Union, after timing contestants for an hour, estimated that the couples were walking approximately forty miles a day.[31] Each elimination tightened the contest around fewer contestants. In the face of the defeat of their competitors, remaining couples seemed to lurch between the power of endurance and the vulnerability of defeat.

By the ninth day of the contest, the remaining twenty couples were referred to as "iron horses."[32] Even so, they made desperate attempts to stay awake. Joseph Tartore instructed his partner Helen Schmidt to sock him in the jaw if he began to get groggy or to entertain the idea of dropping out of the contest. Several times Helen had to comply with his wish, but ultimately her efforts were to no avail. Tartore slipped to the floor and did not respond to strong tonics or punches. The team was eliminated.

Vera Campbell also tried to save her drooping partner, Dave Auerbach, with physical force. When it looked as though Auerbach were going to give up, Campbell kicked his shins, ankles, and feet. Before long her own feet could not take the added abuse of kicking her partner, and Vera had to resort to punches to his chin and jaw.[33] On the tenth day of the dance marathon, however, Auerbach was jolted awake by an unexpected event. The deputy sheriff from Rockland County, New York, had arrived with a warrant for his arrest and would not reveal the nature of the charge. Luckily for Auerbach, Crandall was able to intervene by having Auerbach's father post a bond ensuring his son's appearance in court when the contest was over.[34] Was this just another of Crandall's promotional tricks, or was it a real situation that threatened the natural course of the contest? The question was never answered.

Curious symptoms emerged as a side effect of staying awake for days at a time. The most commented upon were hallucinations, popularly known as going "squirrelly." A contestant would imagine that she or he was actually somewhere else, or that something was happening that was not. Some contestants had imaginary conversations; others tried to climb stairs that did not exist. On the tenth day of dancing, Jack Mortimer of Couple Number 42 complained that large sums of money were missing from his tent. While on the dance floor he protested that a legion of pickpockets was pursuing him. His partner, Billy Rogers, tried to dispel his hallucinations with short punches to his face, but around

1 p.m. Mortimer ran out of the Garden in pursuit of the thieves. He was disqualified for leaving the arena.[35] Meanwhile Della Kennie of Couple Number 91 was picking imaginary flowers and pinning them on her partner, Victor Tomie of Newark. She plucked from shoetops, from nonexistent rosebushes, and from the air overhead. Like Jack Mortimer, Della was at the end of her rope. When the tugboat whistle blew after one of the rest periods, she could not make it back to the floor, and the couple was eliminated.[36]

There was also a grim exchange between Ollie Goss and Alois Bruhin, Couple Number 45. Ollie had begun to scream every time she looked her partner in the face. After repeated attempts to push Alois's face out of her field of vision, she collapsed, and the couple was eliminated after 206 hours and 25 minutes of dancing.[37]

Attrition at the Madison Square show was very rapid. Just one day after the marathon opened, thirty-five couples dropped out. The chief cause was stiff muscles and sore feet.[38] By the evening of the second day only 66 couples, half of the 132 that had started, were left on the dance floor.[39] The dancers were tired. One girl had slept with her head resting on her partner's shoulder but kept her feet moving to avoid elimination. An orchestra helped liven things up, and "extras" were brought in to do specialty dances.

On the eleventh day of dancing only fourteen couples were left on the floor. Both the crowd and the contestants expected a new world record. Much to their disappointment, news came during the course of the day that dancers at the Academy Theatre in Pittsburgh had broken the record of 262 hours and set a new mark of 303 hours. The final three couples dancing in the Pittsburgh show had not given up until Dr. Daniel E. Sable, the chief surgeon of the city's Safety Department, declared them unfit to continue.[40]

Some curious editors from the *Nation,* who had been following the coverage in the *New York Times,* decided to go see the "Dance Derby of the Century" for themselves. They were sorely disappointed. After quoting at length from several *Times* editorials, the editors of the *Nation* summarized their experience as follows:

Reading about the stirring incidents aroused our editorial curiosity and we decided to have a look. We did. What a cruel disappointment. Nothing exhilarating happened for our benefit. It was as dull as a six-day bicycle race. The couples did not even dance—except occasionally. Mostly they just walked around the floor. And often they stopped to take a drink, to chat with friends among the spectators, to have a facial massage or shampoo. At such times they merely shifted their weight from one foot to another so as not to be declared out of the contest. Evidently the reporters for the daily newspapers had better luck or better imaginations than we had.[41]

Shortly thereafter, Assistant District Attorney Ferdinand S. Pecora of New York City informed the public at the Garden show that marathons were forbidden under Section 832 of the penal code. This, Pecora said, made the management liable to prosecution if any citizen complained. Section 832 had been enacted during the six-day bicycle races. It forbade endurance contests allowing less than twelve hours of rest in a twenty-four-hour period. No one took the district attorney's information to heart—at least not right away—but it did intensify interest in the outcome of the show.[42] Despite the new world record, and the threat of prosecution, thirteen couples made it to the twelfth day. By then word of the district attorney's position had gotten out, and Winifred Barry, a "leading lady in a Broadway melodrama of horror," had decided to complain. Although Barry was photographed with a summons in her hands, no one knew exactly what she was complaining about. Whatever her objections, the general public began to believe that Crandall's contest could be seriously threatened by the authorities. Then again, there is the possibility that it was all a ploy. Crandall had not expected the show to last as long as it had. There had been some talk of trying "to dance the dancers down" by shortening the length of the rest periods. Crandall had to find a way to protect his profits by ending the contest before the ticket sales fell too low to cover costs.[43]

The "Dance Derby of the Century" was both a celebrated center of nightlife with a rich clientele and a stopover for the struggling poor. It was no different than the city at large. "Perhaps there had always been two New Yorks. The sparkling mecca of the polished rich and the slum town of the struggling poor. A community blessed by education, ease, and style, and another of narrow loyalties and broad hatreds. A metropolis of joy and beauty and spirit, and a devouring, ruthless city of the scarred and desperate at rope's end."[44]

Crandall's show partook of both faces of the city. In 1928 the inebriation of New York City was palpable. With Jimmie Walker as mayor the city had a model defender of urban nightlife at the helm. About political reformers he quipped, "A reformer is a guy who rides through a sewer in a glass-bottomed boat."[45] Walker's wealth, insouciance, and vaudeville singer wife, Janet Allen, made him the symbol of the moment and helped establish the tone of the city. (He later fell in love with a twenty-three-year-old actress, Betty Compton, and moved into a suite at the New York Ritz to live with her. The press did not report what they knew.)[46] Among his achievements were the legalization of boxing matches and Sunday baseball games.[47]

Despite the hedonistic norms of the 1920s, unemployment was a problem. Although exact unemployment figures for the period are not available because government statistics were not collected, estimates of nationwide unemployment between 1923 and 1928 range from 5.3 percent to 13 percent.[48] Americans still had a longer workweek than workers in other industrialized nations and ranked with the underdeveloped nations of China and India in allowing women and children to work at night.[49] Prosperity, however, was also very real. Between 1919 and 1929 the number of motorcars in the United States grew from 7 million to more than 23 million.[50] In large cities like New York, department stores made unprecedented profits. Retail shops featured an opulent atmosphere and offered easy credit. Seats on the stock exchange went for as high as $625,000. The contestants at Crandall's marathon took part in the atmosphere of propsperity by abandoning themselves to the "crazy competition for getting and spending money."[51]

In this atmosphere, Crandall's marathon succeeded by exploiting the contradictions of the city. Society people, stage stars, and nightclub performers rubbed shoulders with those still trying to make it. It was a time of enormous contrasts. The glamor of urban nightlife rubbed up against the horror angle of much marathon reportage and made for a contest that was celebrated for its indignities. On June 30 the health commissioner closed the show at 2 p.m. claiming it was a risk to the contestants' health. The $5,000 prize money was not awarded, but each of the sixteen remaining contestants was given a small sum at a party in their honor three days later.[52]

Three

FOR NO GOOD REASON

It cannot be denied that the urge that packs arenas for the knock-out punch or the race track for the harrowing spill resulting in death is the motivating force behind this thing called walkathon. The contestant is exalted to the position of combination gladiator and night-club entertainer.

Promoter Leo Seltzer, 1934

By 1931 the Depression had struck deep, and dance marathons took on a much darker cast. What had been light-hearted entertainment became a contest of survival. At least this is the modern perception of dance marathons, as expressed in the film *They Shoot Horses, Don't They?* (1966), an adaptation of the American existentialist novel of the same title, written by Horace McCoy in 1935.

The Depression did more than change the nature of dance marathons; it also determined how they were understood and remembered. The Depression clearly showed that the prosperity of the 1920s had been limited to a small segment of the population. Those whose wealth survived the stock market crash of 1929 were not necessarily willing to help the unemployed. The country that held out the hope that every man and woman could live a prosperous life was faced with image after image that refuted that ideal. Shantytowns grew up on vacant lots in

Annie Oger and Clyde Hamby dance a specialty dance at a small town dance marathon. (Photo from the collection of George Eells)

cities; men sold apples on street corners; a drought swept parts of the country, resulting in the loss of thousands of head of livestock; families were left without food and shelter. Dance marathons during the Depression appealed to the sense of loss and desperation that resulted from these events.

Yet dance marathons did not simply duplicate the terrible reality of the Depression in their structure. Rather, within a theatrical frame, they tried to negotiate the onerous circumstances in which many Americans found themselves.

Dance marathons during the Depression were part of a culture of poverty. They relied on an audience that was out of work and on contestants who were willing to work for very little. Together the two groups collaborated in an event that, if it did not exorcise tensions in the culture, at least laid them bare. The contradiction between the ebullient Americanism of the red, white, and blue bunting that decorated many marathon halls, on the one hand, and the overblown pronouncements of promoters addressing a population of disinherited, jobless, and sometimes homeless men and women, on the other, was not resolved. It was the modus operandi of the entertainment.

Promoters advertised Depression-era dance marathons as "walkathons."[1] By changing the name, they avoided the bad reputation of earlier marathons and were able to attract new audiences. Walkathons were a more elaborate version of the older dance marathons. They featured showmanship and special entertainments—comedy sketches, weddings, mock weddings, elimination contests, and mud wrestling—in addition to endurance dancing and the grim drama that came with staying awake for days on end. Following Milton Crandall's Madison Square Garden show, the "Dance Derby of the Century" (see chapter 2), Depression-era dance marathons increasingly mixed the fiction of theater with real life. The boundaries between what was performed—planned, rehearsed, and presented within the "quotation marks" of theater—and the real contingencies of the event, which forced contestants into dramatic displays of anger, anguish, and love, were always blurred. This blurring was exacerbated by increased contact between spectators and contestants. Notes were passed, and occasionally a contestant and a spectator met during a fifteen-minute rest period for fast sex in the parking lot or under the bandstand. With dance marathons lasting weeks and sometimes months, each day of the contest was a new episode in an ongoing narrative about the debilitating forces that made survival so difficult. These forces were represented by the floor judges, the ministers, and the "church ladies" who tried to put a stop to the contests. The contestants were pitted against them, and their performance was, at least in part, about defeating them.

Depression-era walkathons were an amalgamation of social dance, popular music, theater, and sport. Stunts and sketch material came from vaudeville and the theater; body style and movement were borrowed from vernacular dance; jazz rhythms came from popular music; and from sports came competition, gambling, and the concept of the fan. As a writer of the period, Arnold Gingrich, said, "A walkathon without special entertainment features, both in the contest and in addition to it, would be like a horse show without betting. So there are all manner of stunts worked into the contest itself, and a variety of extra divertissements thrown in."[2]

A typical walkathon was staged in a hall swathed in patriotic bunting

Jewell Yohstock and Arnold Ehling are the bride and groom at this cellophane wedding. The anticipation of see-through costumes drew large crowds to this special marathon event. (Photo from the collection of George Eells)

signaling the legitimacy of the entertainment. A long, narrow raised dance floor was installed and sectioned off with some kind of railing, creating a well-defined arena in which contestants were crowded together and placed on display. When the stage floor was not resilient enough, contestants had to cut the toes out of their shoes to accommodate their swollen feet. Bright lights were hung from the ceiling, illuminating both the spectators and the contestants. The overall lighting made clear that the division between them was a matter of theater and suggested that the spectators might just as well be part of the spectacle. At the far end of the stage was the bandstand. On either side were exits, one marked "Girls" and one "Boys," leading to the contestants' rest quarters. The "hospital" had an open side or a glass wall, inviting the audience to view contestants being treated for injuries or exhaustion. Walkathons were a world unto themselves, with their own rules, sets, music, players, spectators, promoters, cooks, floor judges, doctors, and nurses.

Dance marathons made the struggle for survival into something that was performed, something to be achieved through theater. This mimicry resembled a con game in a way that was unique to American culture. Like professional wrestling, also popular during the period,

Old burlesque and vaudeville sketches such as this one kept spectators entertained during the long hours of the contest. (Photo from the collection of George Eells)

dance marathons critiqued the realism so pervasive in American theater. Many dramatic productions in the 1930s asked spectators to pretend that what was happening was real. Dance marathons asked spectators to see that what was really happening was theater, even while enticing them to pretend that it was not. As a contest, dance marathons brought home the actuality of "survival of the fittest." Yet in theatrical terms marathons were parodies of social Darwinism; what spectators actually saw was a spectacle disguised as a contest of survival. Enthusiasts, both on the scene and listening over the radio, became deeply involved. But at the same time they were aware that the performance was a con game. Marathon enthusiast George Eells recounted, "I knew from the first time I saw them they had to be phony, but being part of the crowd stimulated me to the point of pulling for the contestants even when I knew the whole thing wasn't really legitimate." [3] Eells was alluding to the fact that many marathons featured carefully rehearsed displays of heroism and defeat, and also to the fact that the outcome of the

"Frozen alive" was another special entertainment. The contestant entombed in ice
would use a flashlight to signal to the master of ceremonies and medical staff.
(Photo from the collection of George Eells)

contests was usually determined in advance by promoters. Even so, the
unspoken contract between contestants and spectators was that if contestants performed well, spectators would approve by publicly performing their own spontaneous emotional involvement with the contest.

During the Depression dance marathons became big business—for a
few years, almost legitimate business. The formation in 1935 of the National Endurance Amusement Association (NEAA) was an attempt by
promoters to set standards that would govern all endurance shows.
They wanted to protect the industry from one-shot promoters who did
not know anything about putting on a show. These amateurs or shysters
often went into "virgin" towns, made a fast buck, and split before they
paid their debts, stranding the exhausted contestants without prize
money. The NEAA, however, was never able to make dance marathons
into a legitimate business enterprise. The amateurs and crooks constantly
made the headlines, giving all the shows, honest or not, a bad name.

Dance marathons stressed the survival of the fittest yet they parodied
social Darwinism by situating winning and losing as theatre.
(Photo from the collection of Carol Martin)

During the Depression shows generally lasted from six to twelve
weeks and were open twenty-four hours a day. The audience paid from
twenty-five to forty cents for admission, sometimes more for an evening
with special guest entertainment. A band played in the evenings, and a
Victrola churned out popular music during the day. Contestants had to
be in continual motion for forty-five minutes out of every hour, day and
night. A show could start with as many as a hundred contestants but
would dwindle to about twenty couples during the first few days. As
with Crandall's Madison Square Garden show, contestants did not
exactly dance nonstop. They hung on to one another; they dragged
around the floor, shifting their weight from one foot to the other.
"Walkathon" was a better description of what the contestants were actually doing. But at specific times determined by the promoter they also
danced full out, as well as they could, performing such popular dances

as the fox trot, lindy, jitterbug, and tango. The most grueling development was elimination contests in which everyone was required to participate. Pylons were set up on either side of the room, and contestants ran around them in a variety of ways until someone was eliminated by dropping out, falling down, or coming in last.

A core of professional contestants developed in response to the demand for athleticism, showmanship, and special entertainments. Novices ambitious to become celebrities, or at least to become professional entertainers, and a small contingent who thought of themselves as endurance athletes, went from show to show. They learned tricks from one another and worked on sketches and routines that would help them earn extra money from the spectators. As professionals, they worked harder than the amateurs at convincing spectators that they were behaving spontaneously; they became skilled at competing against one another using their rehearsed bits of dance, comedy entertainments, and athletic displays. While stressing their ability to entertain, they also tried to convince spectators that they were doing all this "for the first time." This disingenuous behavior—common in theater, but duplicitous in the frame of an event billed as an endurance contest—accounts for the shame some contestants felt at having participated in a con. Some contestants were especially well suited to a highly regimented environment. "I think there was a strong personality type that was attracted to this kind of thing," George Eells recalled. "I think they would have adjusted just as well to being in jail or being in the army. As a matter of fact, several of them stayed in the army after World War II. They probably would have made good fascists because they were people who took orders. These contestants were like kids; the promoter took care of them and helped them make decisions. He got them out of jail when they were in jail; he helped them if they got into a financial bind. And then he took advantage of them and made lots of money off them."[4]

Most professional contestants did not enter dance marathons to follow rules. They usually felt they had some special skill that might attract some special attention given the opportunity. At age sixteen, Stan West was a tap-dancing street kid in Laconia, New Hampshire, who earned his living selling newspapers. "I'll buy a paper from you if you do a little tap dance," his customers told him. West responded with an unpolished but convincing enough waltz clog.[5] He slowly expanded his repertory, picking up steps he saw performed by vaudeville performers who played the local theater. West entered his first dance marathon in 1932 in Rochester, New Hampshire, hoping it would be an outlet for his talent. But he soon dropped out of the show.

In 1933 West entered another dance marathon, held in Hampden, Maine, at the Paradise Pavilion Ballroom. This event promised $1,500 prize money. He tapped, and his partner, Peggy Worth, sang. They learned to save their best routines for large crowds, and to rest as much as they could during the short breaks. Things were going well until the Hampden police decided that dancing for a paying audience on Sunday was illegal. The show almost closed, but Mr. Curtis, the promoter, was given permission to continue when he promised to keep the audience out on Sundays. Late the next Sunday night, just after the floor judge had blown the whistle to end a rest period, someone yelled, "Fire!" West remembers the trainer sitting him up on his cot. "Let's get moving!" he yelled. "The furnace just blew." [6] Contestants began to scream and ran out of the rest quarters. West yelled for Peggy when he passed the girls' rest quarters but did not see her. Then the lights went out. West grabbed hold of someone's coat and made it outside into the sub-zero weather. "I let go of the stranger's coat and fell face down in the snow. That revived me somewhat. Struggling to my feet, I tried to figure out what to do next. Where was Peggy, I thought, panic stricken. Suddenly, as I stood there about forty feet from the pavilion, the entire building collapsed in a blaze of burning timbers." [7]

West was led away to a nearby house. He heard a list of missing dancers announced on the radio. His name was among them, but Peggy's was not. After a day and a half of dreamless sleep West woke up, thanked the couple who had taken him in, and took the bus home. Peggy had already left town. On his way to the bus he walked up the hill to the ballroom. There was nothing left of the building where three dancers had died. [8] He picked up a small piece of gnarled metal that he keeps to this day.

Shortly thereafter West entered a marathon in Avon, Massachusetts, with another young woman, Margie Bright. They danced ninety-four days and won first prize. They also fell in love and got married after the contest was over. Together they competed in many shows, although not always as partners. [9] This was the beginning of West's life as a professional contestant.

Like other professional contestants West gradually developed a personal style. Promoters sought out the best entertainers, often soliciting them through the "Endurance Show" pages of *Billboard* or writing to them directly when a dance marathon was about to open. June Havoc, Red Skelton, Frankie Laine, and Anita O'Day all worked as professional dancers in marathons.

Other contestants were not serious professionals like West. Many young people entered shows merely to pass the time and dropped out when they had consumed their fill of free food or found something better to do. "Street kids," West recalls, found they "could get off the street like I did. They could get away from a bad environment. It gave them something to do. A lot of them went in just to get coffee and doughnuts. They were dropouts. They would get in, get something to eat for a few days, and then they were gone. Others, like me, were serious about winning the damn money because it was big money." [10]

Local amateurs joined the contest in the hope of winning the prize money—$1,000 to $1,500—or at least to get some food and have a roof over their heads. When asked why they did it, many professionals and amateurs alike replied, "For no good reason." It was an answer that avoided pity and moralizing. It also was an answer that successfully masked with a flippant air the dancers' consciousness about their real reasons for being there.

Whether professional or amateur, performer or spectator, marathon participants were very active in the construction of the genre. Betty Herndon Meyer was just fourteen when she saw her first dance marathon, advertised as a walkathon, in Tulsa, Oklahoma, in 1933. Betty's conventional world consisted of family, church, and school. She had fantasized about life beyond Tulsa. She wanted to become a famous actress. The dance marathon brought Betty's imagination to life. "It was as if [Hollywood] appeared instantly and magically with [the dancers]. . . . Notes were passed back and forth between some of the high school kids and the contestants in the walkathon. One or two of the contestants were supposed to write poetry so the kids would write poems back to them." Betty wrote tentative notes of good luck to a handsome contestant named Jimmie Parker. He responded: "Dearest Red [Betty has red hair] I think you are a mighty sweet girl—I hope I can see you when the walkathon's over—I would like to dance with you at the Playmor—Thanks for rooting for me—'Dancingly yours' Jimmie

Parker." In closing Jimmie included his home address in Chicago, described the length of time the walkathon had been in progress and the number of dancers ("925 hours, 11 couples and 2 girls"), and noted the place ("Tulsa Coliseum Walkathon").[11] The exchange was personal. The rules of the marathon allowed this, even encouraged it.

The passing of notes from contestants to spectators was a calculated ploy on the part of the contestants, known as "working the rail." Contestants worked the rail to solicit the "ringside ladies" who lavished gifts and attention on their favorites. At some shows it was common for a popular contestant to return from the rest period before "showtime"— from 8 p.m. to midnight—to find a cache of presents piled up on the corner of the stage. For Betty and fans like her it was a tender and arousing contact. The titillation kept her coming back, spending twenty-five cents each time for her ticket, even though she never actually met Jimmie. For Betty the marathon at the Coliseum held out the possibility of realizing her desire to know the world beyond her everyday Tulsa even though nothing ever became of her crush on Parker.

Promoter and publicist Richard Elliott maintains that the progression of any show depended on the audience developing sympathy for at least some of the dancers.[12] This feeling was not generated haphazardly. Part of Elliott's job as a publicist involved working as an advance man. He selected the locations for marathons and contacted local businesses to enlist them as sponsors. He checked out local laws governing the assembly of a large number of people in one place, as well as those concerning how long a continual motion contest could last. If the town seemed to have potential, Elliott notified promoter Hal J. Ross, for whom he worked, and they set a date for opening a marathon.

Before the show could begin, a good master of ceremonies had to be found and hired. A good emcee was one who could elicit heat, laughter, and tears from the audience. The emcee was aided by the contestants; as in professional wrestling, performers deliberately cultivated spectators' sympathies in sophisticated ways. For example, some performers played the role of "villains" while others played "innocent victims." Marathon dancers were like professional wrestlers in other ways, as well: they had to be successful at mastering both athletic and performative skills. The athletic skills were different, but the performative skills were the same. Both dancers and wrestlers had to manipulate the audience's attention, exploiting the emotion of the moment. They also had to ensnare spectators in the complicated interface between the real and the performed. Finally, they had to develop convincing personae or characters. These had to be quickly recognizable types that were flexible enough to be elaborated on in personal and idiosyncratic ways.

The brutal tensions in the primitive opposition of villain and victim made for passionate audience involvement. Contestant Chad Alviso, perhaps the most famous villain in endurance shows, was so hated by marathon fans that she had to avoid the perimeter of the ring for fear of being smashed over the head with chairs. The never-smiling Alviso worked with the floor judges to rile spectators to fiery indignation. Her victim more often than not was the feminine "fairhair," a vulnerable ingenue always about to drop from exhaustion. In a typical scenario Alviso would elbow blond Norma Jasper in the ribs at a moment when the floor judge just happened to be looking the other way. Jasper would feign collapse. Spectators tried to intervene by yelling frantically to the judge to disqualify Alviso for foul play. The closer Jasper's knees came to the floor, the more enraged the audience became over Alviso's attack on the seemingly innocent dancer.

The energy and information flowed two ways, from the stage to the house and also from the house back to the stage. Marathon spectators actively participated—physically, mentally, emotionally, vocally, and materially—in the whole event. Professional contestants were confident performers who knew how to bend the audience's emotions in both mundane and extraordinary ways. Audiences responded by trying to implement their own desires. "People yelled to friends, or to the dancers," commented June Havoc. "[They] wept and screamed when a favorite dropped out; fought among themselves. Audience participation indeed."[13] At one show a man was shouting so forcefully at Alviso that he lost control and fell right out of the balcony. Alviso, Jasper, and the other contestants kept on dancing. "We wanted to get the attention off that," Jasper recalled. In a 1939 Chicago show at the coliseum, Al Capone's sister was moved to hand Jasper twenty-five dollars to start a fight with another contestant.[14] By creating "heat" in the audience and then redirecting that energy, Alviso and Jasper proved their ability as performers.

By the end of each evening, performers accumulated debts of revenge. Would Jasper get back at Alviso? Would "justice" come from an unexpected source? Would the other performers protect Jasper, or

Even the floor judge turned his anger into a rehearsed theatrical display.
(Photo from the collection of George Eells)

would they align themselves with Alviso? Spectators were drawn into
the moment-to-moment playing out of these possibilities. Some scenar-
ios were resolved; others were left open intentionally, becoming increasingly complex over the duration of the contest.

Serial stories, dubbed soap operas, were one of radio's innovations
during this period. The serials typically focused on daily lives of ordi-

nary people (Ma Perkins) or else mixed drudgery with romance and glamor (Mary Noble). Like the radio serials, dance marathons featured complex narrative structures that typically set forth several unresolved but ongoing story lines, elaborated in daily episodes. They seemed to provide audience members with an intimate glimpse into the lives of the contestants. Movie serials were another favorite form of entertainment in the 1930s. Each episode of a serial ended in a heart-stopping, danger-filled climax. Spectators knew that the heroine or hero would escape— the question was how the rescue would be configured. Dance marathon promoters exploited this same appetite for near disaster averted at the last minute. People returned to dance marathons day after day to be thrilled by threats that would never eventuate in death or serious injury to the heroes or the villains, but which still seemed to contain a sinister potential. The radio serials, the movie serials, and the dance marathons all went on and on, day after day.

What underlay these serial entertainments? Perhaps all of them presented the Depression itself as endless, heartbreaking, but not fatal. Each day people faced familiar crises in their ordinary lives: Would there be enough food to put on the table? Would the head of the household ever find a job? Would the whole family have to uproot and move on? These quotidian questions were "dramatic" during the Depression because people's lives depended on how they were answered, and the outcome was so often uncertain. Marathons and the other serial entertainments dealt with the ability to endure. They exploited the daily grind, exposing the emotional and economic dangers lurking in everyday life, even while celebrating the heroism and perseverance of ordinary people.

"The only thing we have to fear is fear itself," President Franklin Delano Roosevelt told the nation when he took office in 1933 at the nadir of the economic crisis. Roosevelt was the first president to broadcast regularly over radio. His "fireside chats" were yet another kind of serial, in which the president explained New Deal issues and policies to ordinary Americans. Roosevelt used the chats to inform and exhort the public. At the same time, his presence on the radio sanctioned the medium as a vehicle for significant reportage and explanation. The newly won prestige of radio enhanced the image of dance marathons when local stations began broadcasting from the dance floor during the events.

In an elimination ceremony Patsy Gallagher and Dale Thorpe lament the fact that
Chad Alviso and Louie Meredith fell out of the contest. With King Brady at the
microphone the ceremony was designed to milk the audience of cash
for the contestants who were being eliminated.
(Photo from the collection of George Eells.)

Betty Freund, the daughter of a marathon enthusiast, grew up during
the Depression. She remembers her mother's involvement this way:
"My mother was obsessed with marathons. They were broadcast from
over the floor at least two times daily on the local radio station. . . . One
was early in the morning, and one was at noon. My mother always listened and had her favorite couples. I went one time and just remember
it being sleazy and depressing. But my mother would take a meal and
stay all day."[15]

Depression dance marathons paralleled serial radio's narrative pattern of crisis and recovery.[16] The twist in the marathon was that recovery did not necessarily mean the triumph of good. If, for example, the
contestants did not generate enough excitement to guarantee a big

house the next night, the floor judge could raise the stakes. The floor judges were much like referees at sporting events in that they made sure contestants followed the rules of the contest. One crucial difference, however, was that they often wielded their power unfairly by harassing the contestants. Blowing a shrill whistle in a contestant's ear, flicking wet towels at tired and swollen legs, and making the "weak ones" work harder were all stock ways to create "cheap heat." At one show a burly judge named Jim "King Kong" Coffee, known as one of the best floor judges in the business, made the spectators so angry that he had to be escorted to his hotel by eight policemen. Because the judge's power was not readily assailable, audiences found it easy to hate him. From the spectators' point of view, the "wicked" contestants like Alviso were not the only villains involved in the contest—villains also controlled the event.

On December 10, 1933, at the Tulsa show that Betty Herndon Meyer was attending, Jimmie Parker and his partner, Helen Leonard, along with three other couples, had to run a 60-minute, 105-lap race in a figure-eight pattern around two pylons set at either end of the dance floor. This kind of race, called a "grind," was just one of many exotic and torturous elimination features. Others included "zombie treadmills," "back-to-back struggles," "hurdles," "circle hotshots," "heel and toe races," "dynamite sprints," "duck waddles," and "bombshells." All of these events were designed to eliminate contestants. Each had its own rules that put the contestants through their paces in various ways. During the zombie treadmill couples were blindfolded and lights were dimmed. In dynamite sprints couples could be taped together or required to run backwards. If a couple failed to make the jump in hurdles they were required to run extra laps. Elimination features created a special urgency about survival, constructing a crisis in which all could not end up well. Someone had to be eliminated.

Dreary repetition punctuated by crises was a good metaphor of the seemingly endless Depression. The "kids" in the Tulsa show, as the emcee called them, had begun dancing and walking forty-five minutes out of every hour, twenty-four hours a day, on October 3, more than two months earlier. The daily accounts of the show, called "dope sheets" after horse-racing broadsides, looked more or less like newspapers. There were headlines, feature stories, and general news items. The December 11 dope sheet reported that practically all the

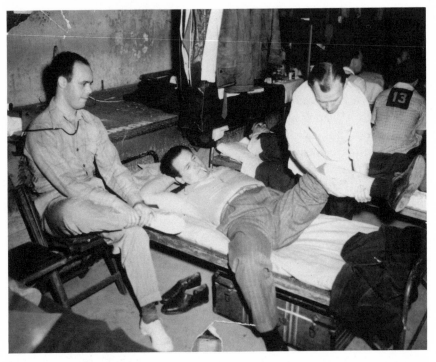

A contestant gets a rub down in the "boys'" rest quarters.
(Photo from the collection of Carol Martin)

contestants had had to step out of the race briefly for medical attention. Jimmie Parker and Helen Leonard, one of the crowd's favorite couples, were having an especially tough time. Jimmie's feet were said to be a solid mass of blisters, and Helen's ankles were on the verge of collapse. When a grueling grind failed to eliminate anyone, Allen "Frankenstein" Franklin, the floor judge, turned up the heat with a special announcement about the next evening's entertainment. The following night both "girls" and "boys" would have to run a race of fifty-five laps. In addition, there would be a special "surprise" for the girl contestants that would eliminate at least one of them. Members of the audience were angry at the thought of the contestants having to surmount yet another obstacle, but at the same time the prospect excited them. The economic realities of the Depression had emotional ramifications that intensified this kind of communication between contestants and spectators. According to Elliott, "Now people came to see them die. That's an overstatement. But they came to see them suffer, and to see when they were going to fall down. They wanted to see if their favorites were going to make it. That was all part of it. It was Depression entertainment."[17] For Elliott, dance marathons were a cruel struggle for survival that brought either glory or despair, and very little in between.

"For forty cents, on any evening, you will see more knockdowns than a fight fan will ever see for forty dollars," wrote Arnold Gingrich in *Esquire* magazine. "For that same forty cents, you will hear as much poor singing and as much low humor, as the frequenter of cabarets will get for a separate investment of dollars ten to forty. For forty cents, if you are cold and lonely and out of a job on a raw winter's night, you join an audience composed of people who appear to have every right to feel as wretched as yourself, and with them you get the thrill of being able to feel sorry for someone."[18] The passion and sorrow that dance marathons aroused in both fans and dancers were emotions spent, at least in part, on the doubtful chances of their own survival.

Spectators kept coming back or tuning in on the radio to follow their favorites through hours of glory and despair. Dope sheets and broadcasts gave marathon fans the opportunity to keep up with what was going on even if they could not attend every day. They also gave management the opportunity to build up and exaggerate the previous night's events. In Winslow, Illinois, where most townspeople did not have radios, the local telephone operator each morning placed a call to the Freeport Walkathon management twenty miles away and then rang her customers with the news about how Winslow's favorite couple was doing.

One of the ways promoters attempted to sustain interest in marathons was to try to arouse spectators on a visceral level. One favorite method was to have "country store" nights. On these evenings, a special drawing was held that rewarded some spectators with bags of groceries. At a time when many stood on bread lines, food was an obsession, and the prospect of winning a supply of groceries was tantalizing indeed. For those who could afford it, every marathon had a refreshment stand that sold hotdogs, popcorn, and soda. Sometimes spectators brought their own food and drink. In the afternoons the "ladies' crowd" often arrived with picnic baskets; the evening crowd was fond of hip flasks.

On average contestants ate three meals and four snacks a day in front

A table was set up on sawhorses so that contestants could eat their meals
while dancing. They were required to keep shifting their weight or
picking up their feet during all meals. (Photo from the
Dance Collection of New York City Public Library, Lincoln Center)

of the spectators. A tall sawhorse table was placed in the center of the
dance floor for each meal. Because contestants were required to keep
moving, shifting their weight from foot to foot as they ate, the table was
high enough so they would not have to bend over to eat. A favorite trick
was to feign falling asleep while eating. A contestant's face would plunk
down into a bowl of oatmeal, making the audience roar with laughter.

Despite these crowd-pleasing antics, the meals themselves were real
and often carefully organized. In their 1929 *Marathon Guide,* Dr. Everett
Perlman and G. W. Nelson published a sample menu:

7:00 a.m. Breakfast
One-half grapefruit
Boiled oatmeal (sweetened with syrup)
One soft-boiled egg
2 slices of whole wheat toast (buttered)

Country store night was a popular way to attract spectators to a dance marathon during the Depression. (Photo from the collection of George Eells)

10:00 a.m.
Cookies
Glass of Milk

12:00 Lunch
One cup of soup (puree or thickened soups)
Vegetable salad with oil dressing
Cottage cheese
Two slices of whole wheat buttered bread

3:00 p.m.
Apples
Oranges
Celery

6:00 Dinner
Soup
One slice of meat loaf
Small baked potato

Cabbage with oil dressing
Two slices whole wheat buttered bread
Milk

9:00 p.m.
Apples
Oranges
Celery
Cookies

12:00 midnight
Whole wheat sandwich of jelly or relish
Black coffee

3:00 a.m.
Celery
Apples
Cookies
Black coffee[19]

The Marathon Guide is a short book of ten chapters designed to set the public record straight about the nature of dance marathons and also to teach the proper care of the human body at such events. Before writing the book Perlman, then a medical student, observed three marathons of varying lengths (320 hours, 670 hours, and 1,448 hours) held in the Minneapolis area. In the introduction, he stated that his method was scientific, since it was based on observation. He exhorted readers to listen to the "unbiased opinions of medical men who were attached to dance marathons" (and who were probably paid by the promoters to be there) and whose opinions were based on scientific principles. In his book Perlman described the ailments of marathon dancers and prescribed treatments for them.

After discussing proper diet and the effect of marathoning on the heart, muscles, circulation, posture, stomach, and upper respiratory tract, Perlman cautioned that the most common problem was to keep the contestant awake after a few days of dancing. One advantage of the dancers' extreme exhaustion, he noted, was that it permitted the doctor to perform painful procedures, such as incision of abscesses, without using anesthetics. Lack of sleep, however, could lead to strange symptoms: "Many cases of rambling and incoherent speech coupled with extraordinary flights of fancy were found among the drowsy people."

The presence of medical staff both reassured spectators and
teased them with the possibility that serious injuries could happen.
(Photo from the collection of George Eells)

But according to Perlman, hallucinations were not an occasion for
alarm, merely an interesting part of marathons. Some seemed to him to
be pure showmanship. His observation of contestants picking up imaginary articles from the floor, for example, led to the following explanation: "As this was more noticeable and most prevalent in those who
were the recipients of frequent cash showers from the audience, it was
supposed that the basis of their 'picking daisies' was pecuniary only."[20]
Picking daisies did in fact become a favorite way for performers to feign
delirium.

Authentic delusions caused one woman to be disqualified from the
contest, when she apparently saw a roomful of men with guns waiting to
shoot her. After a night's rest under sedation, however, she remembered
nothing about the previous evening. When questioned, she confided to
Perlman that her husband had not wanted her to enter the marathon,

and she admitted that perhaps her delusions were really an expression of her concern about her husband's wishes. If he were worried about her mental condition, she reasoned, he could not be angry with her. Perlman also observed several men who were disqualified from contests when they jumped over the railing surrounding the dance floor. When questioned, the men said that the action was involuntary and that they did not know why they had done it. One man, after having jumped over the railing, turned around with a smile of accomplishment only to break down and sob moments later when he realized that he was disqualified.[21]

Delusions of persecution, hysteria, sudden lapses of memory or reason, "goofiness," and "marathonitis" were among the problems that Perlman discussed. "Goofiness," Perlman cautioned, was a malady that could strike anyone on the marathon floor—dancers, trainers, doctors, nurses, managers, or judges. A weak mind, poor memory, and little ability to concentrate were the symptoms. Once goofy, Perlman advised, anyone in a position of authority should drop out because of the possibility of making too many unfair decisions.[22] "Marathonitis" could affect dancers, trainers, and even spectators. Stated simply, it was an obsessive desire on the part of a dancer, trainer, or spectator to dance in, train a contestant for, or watch a marathon. Perlman concluded with a neutral medical appraisal: "It is possible that these derangements are indicative of future mental illness or nervous disorders or it may be that they are merely fleeting signs of an abused mechanism. In any case it will be interesting to watch the behavior and the mental accomplishments in the future of marathon dancers."[23] Perlman was aware of the possibility that what he was witnessing was part theatrical as well as part physical and part mental.

Perlman was right to observe that dancers were really walking, dancing, eating, sleeping, and being injured in full view of the audience. Added to this was the additional indignity in the public presentation of private rituals of grooming, courting, and receiving medical care. There was even a special event called "cot night" in which the cots from the rest quarters were brought out and placed along the perimeter of the dance floor. On these occasions contestants no longer had fifteen minutes of privacy every hour. They were "on" all the time—except for emergency medical treatment and trips to the toilet. Their personal rituals of rest were exposed to the voyeurism of spectators. At the same time, however grotesquely real "cot night" was, it was a performative

convention of dance marathons and was thus under the control of promoters and contestants.

Chance events also ruptured the distinction between the fictional and
the real. Dale Cross, an armed bank robber, once decided to hide out at
a contest at the Playmor in Kansas City. He joined the show as a contestant and danced along with everyone else until someone in the crowd
recognized him. Suddenly the walkathon was swarming with plain-
clothes detectives who whisked Cross away during a rest period.[24]
Thus, marathons were a place where exciting things really did happen.
The dramatic entanglements of the contest were propelled by the conditions of real life, which continually invaded them. Theatrical illusion
was always invigorated with an infusion of real life.

While chance added accidental drama, cruelty was an inevitable element of marathons. Dr. Perlman told this cautionary tale: "A girl was
dancing with a young man. The doctors discovered that she was crying,
and the investigation revealed that great areas on the upper part of
her body were black and blue from his pinching, particularly around
the chest. This couple was disqualified immediately and the girl placed
under a physician's care. We mention this because the reader may have
a daughter or sister under the same circumstances, and it may be said
that the dancers must be watched very closely."[25]

Pain was individual, but time was collective. Huge cardboard timecards marked the hours the marathon had been in progress. Hours
passed into days, weeks, and months. Shared by all, time was indifferent to the comings and goings of spectators and the decreasing number
of contestants. The timecards marking the hours danced were simply
scoreboards. At least three different temporal rhythms came into operation in any marathon: the short, sporadic, and intense periods of crisis
and combat; the longer rhythm of the marathon itself, extending into
weeks and months; and the finale, when rest periods were cut and
elimination features were held one after another to ensure a swift end to
the event. For spectators, the marathons alternated between focus on
individual heroes, comics, and villains, and the overall experience of
participating in an implacable, unstoppable event. The event continued
until all except one person or one couple was exhausted, used up, consumed. Only this couple—and the spectators—survived.

Attending a contest that had been in motion for five days was different from attending one that had been operating for two months. The
longer the contest was in progress, the higher the stakes. Bets changed

hands between spectators more rapidly when the contestants "worked heat." Conversely, the more the spectators had at stake, the more the contestants were likely to create heat. In addition to betting, at any given moment a spectator could publicly send a five-dollar or ten-dollar bill up to the master of ceremonies with a specific request attached. Although the emcee solicited these requests both directly and indirectly, he did not usually have total control over them. A spectator could ask, for example, that the clumsiest team on the floor perform a waltz or that the mousiest girl with the squeakiest voice sing a sexy song. Contestants usually complied with invitations of this kind. To decline would have displeased the management. Most contestants knew when there was a joke behind the request and played to it accordingly. Seasoned contestants learned how to titillate the fantasies of the spectators. In Jasper's words, "we were professionals: we knew exactly what we were doing."[26]

Others were not so sure. Hazel Dietrich, described by George Eells as "a fat girl with a pretty face who couldn't run or entertain," was authentically shy about going up to the microphone. To the crowd's delight, the master of ceremonies would call Dietrich to the bandstand and explain to her that the management had advertised the show as athletic entertainment. "So, Hazel, you have to contribute by doing a dance or singing a song." Hazel refused until the emcee threatened to expel her from the contest. During the whole exchange he was consciously leading the audience to sympathize with Hazel because it was good for the show. When set up by an adept master of ceremonies, the audience responded to entertainments such as Hazel's song with generous "silver showers," a barrage of coins tossed onto the dance floor. Even though the master of ceremonies essentially had forced Hazel to entertain, he had also forced her, in spite of herself, to win a lot of money.[27]

Occasionally a gifted performer turned a request into a creative venture of his or her own. In a 1928 marathon at the Manhattan Casino, spectators had identified the expert dancers in the crowd. The audience created on-the-spot competitions by sending up five-dollar or ten-dollar bills as prizes for the best specialty dance. As a result, George "Shorty" Snowden "decided to do a breakaway; that is, to fling his partner out and do a few solo steps of his own." The audience roared its approval. Later, when asked what dance he had been doing, Snowden replied,

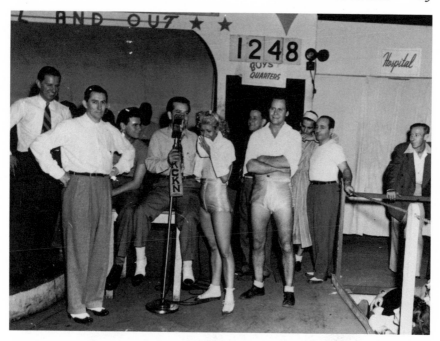

Calling contestants to the microphone whether or not they wanted to come was
the privilege of the master of ceremonies, Hal Brown. Standing on either
side of Brown are King Brady, Patsy Gallagher and her partner Dale Thorpe.
(Photo from the collection of George Eells)

"The lindy"—reportedly coining the name of the famous vernacular
dance.[28]

The power of purchase gave spectators a feeling of superiority. They
got what they requested and, as a result, were better off than the contestants who had to comply with the strong and fickle emotions of the
crowd. Havoc maintained that "breeding, religion, culture—or lack of
it—could not explain the avid interest of the spectators. Their behavior
becomes significant only as a sign of the times. They were drawn to us
by the climate of cruelty in the world. Our degradation was entertainment; sadism was sexy; masochism was talent. The passion they spilled
over us lit up an entire city." [29]

The array of competing personality types was a show in itself. Eells,
who attended his first marathon in his hometown of Freeport, Illinois,
in 1932, when he was eight years old, retained clear memories of the

Master of ceremony Eddie Begley with Billy Willis.
(Photo from the collection of George Eells)

endurance shows he saw from then until 1952. "It was a heightening of what you find in ordinary society, because it was all enclosed in one room." [30] There were always colorful individuals on display. Eells liked to recall a contestant known as Al (a pseudonym for Phil Arnold) who had been institutionalized several times. When Al's behavior got out of control, he pulled out his commitment papers and shouted, "Don't bug me! I'm crazy and I've got the papers to prove it." [31]

Eells, like many others, was drawn in by the marathons. The ideology that held dance marathons together was "get the audience involved." The relationship between the audience and the contestants—exacerbated by, and entwined with, the desperate economic conditions of the

Having once been institutionalized Phil Arnold used to chide, "I'm crazy and I've got the papers to prove it." (Photo from the collection of George Eells)

Depression—formed the nexus of successful marathons. Eells recalled, "As a kid, even though I didn't know rationally what was going on, I knew intuitively that these [the contestants'] were lives in turmoil."[32] As Depression entertainment, marathons displayed and critiqued popular theories of social Darwinism, which asserted that every person had to struggle to gain and keep his or her place in the social hierarchy. The dancers were struggling, but they were also performing. The contest was about struggle, but the theatrics were about playing with the struggle and converting it into entertainment.

Four

Private Fantasy and
Public Ambivalence

The two remaining couples have reached the two ex-
tremes. Mary's warm affection for her lamb is matched
only by Doris' cool indifference to the watermelon king,
and the boys' reaction to their partners' emotions are
much the same, calm acceptance with an occasional
response, each in his own way. But which will last the
longer? The girl who is dancing because she won't fail
her partner or the girl who won't let her partner out-
dance her?

Anonymous newsclipping, early 1930s

Dance marathons varied in tone from day to day and from contest to contest, but certain recurring themes and images unify
the short history of this popular entertainment. Among these
themes, the question of women provoked the most passionate debates
and discussions.

Marathons played out private fantasies and public ambivalence concerning who women were, where they belonged, and how much social,
sexual, political, and economic autonomy they were entitled to. Certain questions came up again and again. Were women really equal to or
stronger than men? What would happen to men if this were true?
Should young women be allowed to perform in public day after day,
night after night? What kinds of regulations were needed to protect
women from the undesirable influences that were a part of dance marathons? Posed another way, these questions were about the negotiation

of power between men and women, the female body on display, and the strategies of reformers who wanted to regulate marathons. These questions became central to the controversy about the role of women in dance marathons and, by extension, in society.

During the 1920s men and women adapted to changing sexual relations by relegating them to home and leisure, while the sobriety of the mostly male world of work remained intact.[1] Much has been said about women working during World War I, but at the height of women's employment only 5 percent of the women working had not previously been in the labor force. During the war women were promoted to higher paying jobs that demanded a higher level of skills, only to be demoted once the men returned. Cultural heroines, such as the streetcar operators in Cleveland, were faced with men, who had returned from war, striking to protest the women's continued employment.[2] Women did not improve their position in the labor force in the 1920s or the 1930s. New values concerning gender and sexuality were played out in public entertainments where they were viewed as private rights.[3] Meanwhile, the economic order remained the same.

At dance marathons, one of the first hotly debated questions was who could last longer, "boys" or "girls." Whether it was fabricated by the press or arose from the fans, this question neatly linked gender to the expendability of the body. As narrative dramas of physical urgency, dance marathons consumed their contestants. For all that was said about "lasting the longest" and breaking records, the body in motion at these entertainments was first and foremost exhaustible, capable of being entirely used up, worn out. Personal needs and conditions—hunger, sweat, sleep, wakefulness, bodily functions, pleasure, and sexual desire—that were never actually seen in other performances of the day, were on display throughout marathons and, in fact, were one of their attractions. The frailty and glory of the body, its physical needs and intimate desires, were the focus of each performance. Playing out physicality as a drama of gendered opposition was a way of framing public displays of what was usually thought of as private. It was also a way of asking questions about the rapidly changing relations between men and women in the 1920s and 1930s.

Men and women dancing together, remaining physically close in public for days at a time, was disturbing enough. The notion of men and women dancing in competition with one another, either as couples

Couples like this one made the press and spectators speculate that women were as strong as men. (Photo courtesy of the Library of Congress)

or as soloists, was even more unsettling. Unsettling because it meant that gender roles were being revised, especially as they were played out by the heterosexual couple. After the passage of the Volstead Act of 1920, which made illegal the possession and consumption of alcoholic beverages and marked the beginning of the era of Prohibition, dancing seemed to become more licentious. Reformers had been involved in trying to control leisure entertainments, but after Prohibition individual rebellion against this control became more urgent. With the proliferation of speakeasies, rebellion often took the form of illegal drinking in a nightclub environment.[4] As a result, dancing quickly became associated with the illicit pleasures of the night. Men and women had been dancing physically close together at least since 1910—the hesitation waltz, the Argentine tango (both banned by the Federation of Women's Clubs in 1914), the bunny-hug, the foxtrot, the turkey trot. In the 1920s dance, coupled as it was with the celebration of personal freedom and the possibility of illegal drinking, came to represent a transgressive pastime.

In the earliest dance marathons contestants competed individually. Each contestant was accompanied by a series of partners who tried to help him or her break the world record. A partner, or a set of partners, could help a contestant win without receiving any personal recognition for themselves. Concerning these early contests an enthusiastic journalist commented in the *Literary Digest*, "The most interesting fact about this pedomania is the superior staying power and perhaps grit of the female contenders. They commonly tire out half a dozen Tom, Dick and Harrys, their partners in the exhausting shuffle. The 'gentler sex', the 'weaker sex' have almost been banished from print already. In the interest of truth, it now appears, these phrases should never again evade the blue pencil."[5] The writer's perception was that female contenders were creating new possibilities for women. His barely concealed fear was that in the face of female power and grit men would be reduced to just so many "Tom, Dick and Harrys."

The optimism of this commentary reflected the sentiment of some of the spectators at early marathons. The writer was correct in pointing out that something had changed. "Staying power" and "grit" were very different accolades for the sex that until 1923 had been presented in public entertainments as a mass of lovely, lavishly costumed or partly naked chorus girls serving as the background to song-and-dance numbers.[6] Female contenders at marathons were not graced with the aura provided by theatrical lighting or costuming, nor did they hide anonymously amid a mass of smiling women. They were exuberant individuals, part of the youth culture of the 1920s. Their clothes were straight from daily life. What set them apart was what they did, not how they appeared. Appearing "beautiful" to men could not have been a serious consideration in a contest that demanded hours of sweat and wakefulness. Determination, without benefit of rouge or powder, was what spectators watched.

Accompanying the article in the *Literary Digest* was a list of records. Female soloists—Alma Cummings, Ruth Molleck, Helene Mayer, Magdalene Williams, Madaline Gottschick, Vera Sheppard, and June Curry—accounted for seven of the ten records. These early winners were heroic figures. Their triumphs in competition incited and encouraged other women, even as they competed against one another. As individuals, they demonstrated will and courage in the face of an ordeal. When they danced beyond expectation they demonstrated what was survivable and surmountable: they triumphed over the image of the frail, feminine Victorian body.

Such ideas provoked the press and the public into thinking about just what was happening on the dance floor. Not everyone agreed that a new female power was emerging. There was speculation that the members of the "weaker sex" held most of the endurance records because they were assisted by a succession of strong male partners who exhausted themselves heaving the "girls" around the dance floor.[7]

An unnamed writer for the New York *Evening World* suggested that a "dancemobile" be invented to carry the winner to the finish. This way the women would expend even less energy. "The closing hours of a record-breaking dance revealed how little a 'record' means," he commented. "The dancing partner of the winner dropped out. The reason was said to be the need for fresh partners who would be able to support the winner in her exhausted condition—in other words, to carry her and dangle her feet along the floor." The author then described his suggested mechanical substitute for the thankless job of the male partner. "To inventors we suggest the modification of the tricycle for children, adjusting the seat so that the toes of the dancer just reach the floor. Then attach driving rods from the rear wheels to the ankles to supply power to push the device and dancer about the dancing floor."[8]

A triumphant woman literally standing on her own two feet was too threatening for some people to take seriously. The counterimage that the *Evening World* writer created—women riding around on tricycles with their feet just reaching the floor—is, in some ways, appropriately humorous. Inherent in the commentary was a question well worth considering: what kind of victory was this, anyway? However ironic the observation or amusing the proposed solution, the writer makes his point by deprecating women. To first expose and then further construct female dependence is the writer's real intention. The image of a woman dependently dangling from a manmade contraption, a surrogate for multiple male partners, created the literary illusion that the winning female contestants could not have achieved victory on their own. The notion that a succession of men would serve one woman, enabling her to reach her goal, was equally disturbing in terms of any traditional balance of power. Hence in this imagined scenario of women on tricycles, men disappear altogether. The cleverness of this journalist's insinuation lay in how neatly he circumvented, yet underlined, male participation. In the face of women as champions, this writer was asking, on some level and with a great deal of anxiety, where were the men?

Interestingly, an anonymous writer posed some corollary questions in an article immediately following the one that praised female contestants in the *Literary Digest*. Titled "The Passing of 'The Giants' in the Women's Movement," the article first asked who the new leaders would be. Mary Garrett Hay was retiring from the chairmanship of the New York League of Women Voters, and Carrie Chapman Catt was retiring from the presidency of the International Suffrage Alliance. After determining that new leadership was not in sight, the writer pointed out that it had not yet been determined if women had accomplished everything for which they had been fighting.[9] It would be too easy, although perhaps not entirely untrue, to say that the women who were breaking dance records were the beneficiaries of the work of the suffragists. Suffragism was over when the vote was won. Afterward, class difference and generational conflict continued to separate the groups. The feminist activists of the 1920s were typically middle-class or upper-middle-class women, while marathon dancers typically came from the working class. The activists attempted to mobilize sexual solidarity in order to pursue individual freedom.[10] Solidarity, however, escaped them. The goals of feminist activists in the 1920s were divided between those for and those against protective legislation. Whether women as a class needed to be protected was hotly debated. Women dancing in marathons had their own youth culture that self-consciously held values different from those of the older generation. They pursued the right to enjoy nightlife and entertainment for their own intrinsic rewards. Female marathon dancers were not dancing and winning for their sex, they were doing it for themselves.

At marathons like the 1928 "Dance Derby of the Century" at Madison Square Garden, partners competed as a team; if one dropped out the other was eliminated as well. Because at that time rules were still being formulated, there was always some variation from show to show. Depression-era marathons returned to the model of the divisible couple. Although in the earliest marathons dancers had been able to compete solo, during the Depression dancers always competed as couples. However, if one person in a couple dropped out, there was nothing to prevent the remaining partner from obtaining a replacement from the contestants already in the marathon. If a woman lost her partner, for example, she could solo for a limited amount of time to see if a man would become available from a couple in which the woman dropped out. The couple was composed of components that could be separated and recomposed.

It is difficult to infer much about the views of women who danced in marathons. Too few of their own voices were recorded, at the time or later. With a few exceptions, the excitement surrounding their participation was largely depicted by men. One voice that stands out is that of a young woman who participated in her first marathon in 1934. Identified simply as Jessie by a social worker, she described her experience with her dance partners at an unidentified marathon this way: "We used to sleep standing up. Honest! I've slept for three hours at a stretch moving all the time. At first, I couldn't but after I got tired, believe me, I could. The idea is your partner pushes you around while you sleep if he is a good partner, but some of them are mean. My partners were all good to me. I wore out five of them." She went on to say: "But I was good to them too! They couldn't understand how I could push Jimmy Donahue when he weighed 150 pounds and I weighed only 116. But I did it."[11] She not only did it, she was one of the five winners who danced 112 days with only 11 minutes out of every 90 to rest.

Romance did not dictate the terms of these partnerships. The competition to win the prize money overwhelmed all other considerations. Edna Smith, a one-time marathoner in a 1928 show in Harlem, recalled how she met her partner: "You know I can't remember his name, but I think it was Bill. He was a young man going to school to study law. I didn't know him when I joined. He didn't have a partner, and I didn't have a partner. There were a lot of people just standing around, and they [the organizers] would place you with a partner if you didn't have one. Bill came up to me and asked if I would like to be his partner, and I said all right."[12] So they danced together for 389 hours—16 days— before they fell out of the show.

Yet romance narratives became a part of dance marathons. Especially during the Depression, romances served to reinstate traditional gender

A marathon wedding during the Depression, when many deferred marriage
because of economic instability, held out hope for the future. It also served as
a hiatus in which the tensions of the marathon were temporarily assuaged.
(Photo from the collection of George Eells)

roles. Weddings became a regular attraction at Depression marathons.
They secured the spectacle of romance in the institution of marriage
and declared that men and women each had a role to play. Conferring
a natural and rightful place for men and women in the institution of
marriage served to temporarily defer the anonymity of unemployment
spectators were experiencing. A wedding during the Depression, when
many people deferred marriage because of economic instability, held
out the hope of renewal, thus also assuring links to the past.[13] Typically,
a promoter would ask two individuals, not necessarily a couple, to feign
falling in love so they could be married during the marathon. Brides-
maids were selected, along with best men. The promoter hired a
preacher to conduct the service and planned a wedding celebration that
included everyone at the marathon, spectators as well as dancers, musicians, and judges. Spectators readily brought gifts to the newlyweds.

After the wedding—during which the bride, groom, and wedding party had to keep dancing—more than one couple found the ceremony convincing enough to honor the contract. But most of them got a divorce if, in fact, the service had been authentic.

At the opposite end of the spectrum were the mock weddings, also a regular special entertainment at marathons during the Depression. These events underscored the theatrical convention of locating gender in conflict and opposition. As much as the wedding assuaged anxiety by reestablishing clear gender roles for men and women, the mock wedding proposed that those roles were rooted in hypocrisy and antagonism. The theatrical mission of mock weddings was to deride and parody the traditional bride and groom, as well as to foreshadow the domestic drudgery that would soon be upon them. Typically the groom was dressed as a slob in oversized jacket and pants that resembled a suit exaggerated to look like a clown costume. His appearance was a parody of the authority, sobriety, and security of the traditional male. His bride, sometimes played by a man in drag, was dressed in something that revealed her intention of soon abandoning any claim to beauty. She was disheveled, her train was too long, and she was sexually forward while asserting that she was not about to serve her man: the orderly and neat world of domesticity was not for her, and she made no pretense about it.

The proximity of the sexes in this competitive atmosphere of marathons—unlike athletic competitions where men's and women's events were segregated—begged the question of gender differences. As many of the surviving photographs of marathons show, the heterosexual couple was the organizing theme that promoters of the marathons wished to present to the public. Couples made extra cash by selling photographs of themselves. These souvenir photographs always depicted couples demurely waiting in dance position for the contest to begin. The gender vocabulary of these images was conventional. The man had his arm around the woman, who rested her hand on his shoulder ready to follow his lead. What happened to this couple once the contest began was not depicted in the pictures for sale. Images of disheveled couples, of women who were stronger than men, or of other "revisionist" situations were understood as "news," not as nostalgic souvenirs. These photographs appeared in newspapers or were kept in the scrapbooks of participants and promoters.

The debate in the press about who could last longer was most promi-

The theatrical mission of mock weddings was to deride and parody the traditional bride and groom. In this photograph Jack Stanley is the groom of an unidentified (male) bride. (Photo from the collection of George Eells)

nent when dance marathons first began. As the shows developed into extended entertainments, women's participation was understood from new perspectives. Because dance marathons blurred the boundaries between private and public behavior, women who danced in them were suspect. Some people found morally questionable the willing display of what was traditionally private behavior. Women were even more vulnerable because male promoters, who were willing to exploit women in any way they could, were in control. For example, when promoter Hal J. Ross was trying to persuade journalist Richard Elliott to be his publicist, he took Elliott into the "girls'" quarters to show him around. Elliott later said, "I suppose he was smart in this. It tells you how showmen are sometimes. Well, of course, most of them [the women] were totally naked. I guess he figured he was going to give me a great big thrill."[14]

Souvenir photographs such as this one with its conventional gender
vocabulary depicted couples far from the demands of the contest.
(Photo from the collection of George Eells)

Thrilled or not, Elliott went to work for Ross. He claimed that those employed by Ross "were mainly young people who had nothing else to do or who couldn't find a job." But virtually in the next breath he confided, "A lot of females in the shows were gals off the streets. I remember once in Miami, one of them boasted to me about her life. Quite exciting. . . . She was what they call a 'five way girl.' She could have sexual relations five different ways." [15] There was usually no overt titillation during the dance marathons; the women were fully clothed and were not licentious in their behavior. Still, the economic uncertainty of their situation made women easy targets of male manipulation. Whether or not Elliott's statement was private fantasy, it pointedly summarized public ambivalence.

The frame of the marathons was almost entirely male. Promoters, publicists, floor judges, journalists, musicians, and masters of ceremonies—all were men. Only in this context can we account for Elliott's contradictory statement. Both Elliott's comment and Ross's action of taking Elliott into the "girls'" rest quarters reveal how a male frame of reference attempted to determine and control meaning. Once a woman joined a marathon she was no longer just a "regular" woman. For some, joining was an indication of a woman's financial need, which made her ripe for exploitation, often in unforeseen ways, such as being placed on display as an enticement for a potential publicist. A woman's willingness to take part in a contest could cause her to be viewed as both vulnerable and suspect. Her vulnerability made her the girl next door, someone to cheer and protect. But it also made her suspect because she was capable of being exploited—a potential whore catering to any man's unnameable ("five different ways") desires. Perhaps this was inevitably how women were seen, no matter what they said or did. No matter how heroic or commonplace their pursuits, they were up against cultural definitions of masculinity, femininity, and sexuality. Elliott was testifying that women at dance marathons were read, among other things, in relation to sexuality. The more powerful the women's performance, the greater the imperative of asserting the masculine frame. Women were both emerging and exploited.

The assumption that unites Elliott with the *Evening World* writer who pictured women on tricycles is that women had no agency of their own. They were in the service of men sexually, and dependent on them physically. Neither Elliott nor the writer considered that women were winning because of their own volition or that they might have sexual desires completely apart from the ways and designs of men. Or if Elliott and the journalist did consider women as independent of men, they invoked the dichotomy of "regular" girl or whore to undermine the possibility of female autonomy.

The attitude of Elliott and the newspaper writer was typical. In an article in *Variety*, reminiscing about dance marathons, George Eells described two women dancers: "Take Iris. Lots of people did. Iris was blonde, blue-eyed, petite. She looked as if she ought to be a wedding-cake decoration and swore like a seaman. Rose was a part-time marathoner and a part-time whore. 'When my feet get tired, I go into a [whore] house,' she used to say. 'And when my back gets tired (only she didn't say back), I enter a contest.'"[16]

Certainly some women came into contact with prostitution through the dance marathons, and some prostitutes participated in the contests. According to one man who attended many marathons in his youth, and whose mother was a close friend of both prostitutes and marathoners, "marathon promoters visited regular dance halls looking for young, energetic, attractive talent to recruit. Some promoters were quite unscrupulous and inducted more pliant girls into prostitution, after first seducing them through their affection and loyalty." This was not unusual during the Depression. Some women who would not ordinarily have done so sold sex for economic survival. But instead of committing themselves to a full-time life of prostitution, such women used prostitution as a temporary solution until they could support themselves by other means. The same man added, "When I was a freshman in high school, delivering papers at five in the morning, I encountered a female classmate going to work in a brothel. She was not an exception in those times of Depression."[17]

In the dance halls, speakeasies, and roof gardens of the day, it was sometimes difficult to distinguish the style and dress of respectable women from those of the prostitutes.[18] Dance marathons followed this pattern. Some marathons were relatively free from prostitution, while others presented many opportunities for paid sexual activity. Marathoners called the main place where sex took place the "snake room." Sometimes the snake room was condoned by the management, and sometimes it was not. "This was a situation where you would talk with somebody in the audience and ask them to meet you in a certain place in the rest period," recalled dancer Stan West. "That was the snake room. It was usually a fast situation. But it was more or less a necessity, a pulsating necessity of youth." West continued, "You could also make your own snake room behind the bleachers or wherever. But if you got caught, you would be disqualified. The jealous ones on the floor, the gay ones like Hughie Hendrixson, would go and tell because they figured it would be one less dancer they had to compete against." [19]

West's account typifies the sexual atmosphere of dance marathons. Sexual jealousy, and not just on the part of gay contestants, was part of the marathon for contestants. Sometimes the promoters and the managements knew what was going on, at other times they did not. Sometimes they knew and said they didn't. Given promoters' experience and their control over the shows, most had to be aware of sexual activities. However, generally promoters did not want the sale of sex associated with their shows. The real question was whether they were going to use what they knew to disqualify contestants. In fact, this depended on the promoter's own agenda, including his relationship to the contestants. Favorites and professional dancers were given a great deal of latitude, while others were called for any violation of the rules. But if the law or local reformers showed up at a marathon, a promoter might disqualify even favored contestants for casual sexual contact in order to demonstrate his social rectitude and good will to the powers that be.

Many of the contestants were young and single, and they found sex relatively easy to come by. "Like I say when you're young you're pulsating with a sexual feeling," said West. "You would see some girl that you liked and ask her to meet you outside the tent at rest break and tell her you had only eleven minutes. That was it. A couple of times I went out during the twenty-minute shower period early in the morning. Crazy, isn't it?" [20]

The possibility of contact, from explicitly sexual to simply flirtatious, was real and always in the air. What worried reformers was the close distance between flirtation and sexual contact at dance marathons as well as at other amusements. Members of the Girl's Protective League saw dance marathons from this reformer's perspective. In 1934 Mrs. Ruth Roberts Mix, chair of the Girl's Protective League, sent the *Journal of Social Hygiene* a transcript of a conversation between a protective worker and Jessie, the fresh-voiced young woman quoted earlier, who had recently danced in her first marathon:

"Yes," said Jessie, "I was in a marathon. Sure I liked it! We had a lot of fun. . . . I was in it for 112 days and I won fifth prize which was

$37.50. I thought it would be more when I went in but we made most money on 'sprays' [money thrown to the contestants from the audience for special songs, dances, or sketches]. I picked up $29.00 one night in a spray for me. Did you hear me on the radio? Gee, I never knew I could sing before but one night they gave me a singing lesson for my solo stunt. That was the night they sprayed me for $29.00. . . . No, we never had any time to sleep. . . . We used to sleep standing up. Honest! . . . Rough crowds? No, they're lovely people. And believe me, the management won't stand for any 'monkey business.' We were allowed 15 minutes a day for a hot shower. And every morning the referee took us for a thirty minute walk outdoors."[21]

Mrs. Mix was worried that dance marathons were so stimulating that they would take away a girl's desire to make a living by "honest work." Indeed, earning twenty-nine dollars in one evening had been a big boon for Jessie. She had every intention of entering another marathon as soon as she got some rest. The concept of "honest work" always invoked its opposite, bringing with it those associations with which reformers were really concerned: unsupervised and unregulated leisure, exploitation, and prostitution. One vice led to another. This was not simply a naive conflation cooked up by reformers but one that had been proven by years of experience:

> Where young women saw an aura of sensual pleasure, middle-class observers of commercial halls found immorality, drawing a lurid connection between working girls' recreation and vice. The press was filled with dramatic accounts of innocent daughters tempted by glittering dance halls, seduced and drugged by ruthless "cadets" or pimps, and held against their will in brothels. Beyond the sensationalism, their views had some basis in fact. As historian Ruth Rosen has shown, incidents of white slavery did occur in the nation's largest cities. The Committee of Fourteen, a reform agency formed to battle urban prostitution and vice, sent undercover investigators to [New York's] saloons and dance halls in the 1910s.[22]

What this committee's agents saw were places that provided the opportunity for strangers to make sexual contact. That the activity did not necessarily happen was not the point.

For all that was said about reformers intervening at dance marathons, their presence is not well documented. Although reformers probably figured in the eventual banning of marathons in some cities and towns, movie theater managers were most frequently cited as the greatest enemies of dance marathons. Richard Kaplan, the president of the National Endurance Amusement Association, issued this warning in the June 29, 1935, issue of *Billboard:* "Because the theatre managers are afraid of healthy competition, because they do not want to appear too much in the open in opposition to walkathons, they have enlisted the aid of ministers, societies, and women's clubs. And they pick out the illegitimate show conducted by an illegitimate and ignorant promoter as an example of what the walkathon is, using such a show as their entree into such organizations."[23]

Yet reformers were seen as natural enemies by contestants and promoters alike. Even before Prohibition, reformers were depicted as puritanical. From the vantage point of the youth culture of the 1920s, reformers represented small-town Protestantism, bent on censoring social, sexual, and ethnic heterogeneity and pleasure-seeking urban culture. The young women of this generation consciously perceived their own identities as distinct from their elders.[24] The remains of Victorian mores were not for them. The enthusiasm they felt for female marathon dancers was intensified by contempt for their opposites: women who upheld traditional femininity. "Church ladies" was a euphemism for those women who made it their business to survey and control public leisure entertainments. Church ladies represented attempts to restrict personal liberty.[25] They lobbied civic authorities to ban dance marathons in the interest of moral uprightness. Unlike female dance marathoners who submitted to the marginal authority of male promoters, the church ladies appealed to men with civic power. Although socially motivated, church ladies' concerns were portrayed as nothing more than prudery hostile to sexual expression.

The word *feminism* appeared and came into frequent use in 1910 (the nineteenth-century women's movement did not use the term).[26] Although the term signaled the creation of a modern women's agenda, some of the concerns of the nineteenth-century movement continued well into the twentieth century. Among these was social welfare, in whose spirit many of the church ladies sought to ban marathons. A concern for the well-being of the community, especially for those members of the community with little or no money—most often women— guided their actions. This made little difference to promoters and dance marathoners. Church ladies joined the ranks of the oppressors. To middle-class reformers, working-class dance marathons were an unwelcome addition to the problem of unregulated leisure entertainments.

The idea of the reformer as adversary easily entered the popular narrative of dance marathons. Horace McCoy's 1935 novel *They Shoot Horses, Don't They?* depicts Gloria, an anti-heroine, who knows the conditions of her life are untenable but who can find few alternatives. Unsuccessful in her attempts to get into motion pictures, she joins a dance marathon instead. She is given to displays of temper, and she rages against two members of a women's group who come to the marathon to inquire about a contestant they had heard was pregnant. The reformers intend to inform the promoter that "The Mother's League for Good Morals" has condemned the contest and wants it closed. Gloria confronts them in the promoter's office:

> "It's time somebody got women like you told," Gloria said, moving over and standing with her back to the door, as if to keep them in, "and I'm just the baby to do it. You're the kind of bitches who sneak into the toilet to read dirty books and tell filthy stories and then go out and try to spoil somebody else's fun—"
>
> "You move away from that door, young woman, and let us out of here!" Mrs. Higby shrieked. "I refuse to listen to you. I'm a respectable woman. I'm a Sunday School teacher—"
>
> "I don't move a f— inch until I finish," Gloria said.
>
> "Gloria—"
>
> "Your Morals League and your goddamn women's clubs," she said . . . , "filled with meddlesome old bitches who haven't had a lay in twenty years. Why don't you old dames go out and buy a lay once in a while? That's all that's wrong with you." [27]

As a representation of the kind of hostility that arose between working-class and middle-class women over issues involving leisure, this dialogue is extremely revealing, even if it is a fictional exchange. As Mrs. Higby prepares to leave, she tells Gloria that she should be sent to reform school. Gloria replies, "I was in one once. There was a dame just like you in charge. She was a lesbian." [28]

Gloria's charge that the Mother's League for Good Morals was driven by the members' own prurient interests, rather than the interest of morality, shows just how far middle-class reformers could be from the objects of their concern. By the 1930s, with the commercialization of leisure and consumption, the reformers' task was really hopeless. The whole exchange between Gloria and Mrs. Higby takes place beneath three pictures of nude women tacked to the wall in the promoter's office. The pictures are an indication that this is man's country. A similar attitude was demonstrated by Hal J. Ross when he invited Richard Elliott into the girl's rest quarters to have a look around.

Reformers wanted to protect women from the exploitation that men's control implied. Ironically, despite their differences, reformers joined promoters and some journalists in a common assumption. They believed that left to their own devices women were morally and physically corruptible, vulnerable, and exploitable. Inadvertently, reformers and promoters collaborated in questioning the assertion that women could generate their own moral, physical, and economic power.

This struggle over how to regard women who participated in marathons, and the debate it aroused, remains among the most interesting aspects of these events. Ultimately, the struggle was about power: physical power (who could last longer?), moral power (could women avert or overcome exploitation?), and economic power (was this a place where independent women could earn a living, albeit a meager one?).

Promoters were against reformers intruding on their turf, their own economic interests. The reformers, on the other hand, may have been genuinely concerned about the exploitation of young women, but they were also admonishing them, usually talking down from the position of a superior social class. The power they tried to assume—to determine for all women what was right and wrong—was vehemently rejected by women who were already earning a living, however marginal, on their own.

Whatever might have been transgressive (such as the absolute determination to win) about female participation was potentially subverted by men's control over the marathons. Journalists, promoters, and publicists tried to make sure that women winning dance marathons were contained and secured in the male-dominated world of entertainment. Women winners did not change the economic order. Yet they were admired by some people precisely because they posed a serious challenge to accepted notions of male superiority. The challenge generated a debate that had never taken place in quite the same way.

Men controlled the economics, the staging, and the story line of marathons. Most of the recorded point of view on the events is male.

Although dance marathons, like other leisure entertainments, easily absorbed, proclaimed, and sold the representation of new ideas about sexuality and gender, these representations remained a work of the imagination that became real only for brief moments in the context of the fiction of performance. Yet the impact of the images was noted and recorded by the press, as well as exploited by promoters. And there is no way to measure the extent to which these women may have contributed to the survival of a feminist impulse with their popular performances of endurance.

Women were not completely powerless, at least in relation to audiences. Male culture could not entirely enfold and construct what the women were doing. Women who danced in marathons enjoyed the excitement of the public stage, the glare of the lights, and the approval of the crowds. Morally speaking, they were no better or worse than the men with whom they danced. Their performances of "manual labor" did earn them a certain economic and psychological autonomy. The image of determination they created with muscle and sweat threatened, for a short time, to break some women loose from the status quo. Promoter Ross knew that dance marathons centered on women. He envisioned a time when a woman would regularly play the role of floor judge and "mistress of ceremonies." It never happened—but if it had, who knows what meanings might have been generated?

Five

HAL J. ROSS
CUNNING, SMART, AND SLICK

Never, to my knowledge, has Marathon dancing under
proper conditions done any participant any harm, and in
my opinion is not subject to any criticism, any more than
football, in which each year we hear of broken necks,
backs, etc., or many of the other sports which yearly take
an actual toll of human life. Never, in the four years of
Marathon, has there been fatality, with but one exception,
and that was a non-stop Marathon in which a young lady
dropped dead, and which was the cause of such unjust
criticism of Marathon dancing.

Hal J. Ross, "In the Training Quarters,"
The Marathoner (1929)

The picture of dance marathons created by their promoters is very
different from the one drawn by the contestants. Promoters have
been much maligned because they were the bosses who ran the entertainments and who made most of the money. Although all promoters
were exploitative, some were also serious showmen. They developed
strategies for putting on good shows, paid their debts, and generally became known in the communities where they staged events. Hal J. Ross
was one of these top-of-the-line promoters.

Ross was born on May 16, 1893, in Portage, Wisconsin. As a young
man, Ross worked in the motion picture business until he was sent
overseas in 1918 as a commissioned officer in the 32nd division of
the U.S. Army. After being wounded several times, Ross was eventually placed in charge of army productions; his responsibilities included buying the make-up and costumes used by the soldier-actors.

Hal J. Ross. (Photo from the scrapbook of Richard Elliott)

Upon returning from the war, Ross moved to Chicago, where he worked as a trainer for amateur boxers until he became a partner in a dance marathon in 1928.[1] By 1930 Ross had moved south to Texas to try out his skills as an independent dance marathon promoter. As an active member of the W. B. Williamson Post No. 1 of the American Legion as well as of the Veterans of Foreign Wars, Ross was able to rent American Legion Halls in small towns and gain the sympathy of other veterans. After staging several successful shows in Texas and Florida, Ross set sail for Europe in the spring of 1931 on the *S.S. America*. He remained abroad, staging marathons, until the spring of 1932. He was the only American promoter to stage dance marathons in France and Germany.

Ross was an articulate man who, from the very beginning of his involvement with marathons, was also concerned with the vices that

afflicted the profession. Although he knew well how to manipulate audiences and contestants, he had a sense of propriety. Consequently, he
became a spokesperson for the nascent dance marathon industry and
eventually became a founding member and first president of the National Endurance Amusement Association (NEAA). As president, Ross
tried to unify the rules and procedures of dance marathons by propos-
ing guidelines and urging all promoters to adopt them.

Ross was skilled at attracting the right people to his marathons. Contestants, singers, publicists, and masters of ceremonies readily joined
his events. Important members of the local community lent their
support. Richard Elliott, working as a newspaper reporter in Corpus
Christi, Texas, in the summer of 1930, remembered very clearly how he
became involved with Ross: "To make a little extra money I had been
doing publicity for the modern wrestling promoters. . . . They recom-
mended me [to Ross] to do the publicity for the Corpus Christi marathon which was on a pier out over the water off North Beach. Most
marathon promoters wanted somebody else to share the risk with them.
Ross made a deal with me whereby I would have 20 percent of the show
and would be the publicity person and do the local stuff." [2]

Elliott met Ross fairly early in Ross's career as a marathon promoter.
Previously, Ross had staged relatively small dance marathons in Mexico
City and Harlingen, Texas. He was working up to trying something on
a larger scale. The Harlingen marathon was staged largely to test the responses of a Texas audience. The show was so successful that some
contestants from Harlingen were expected to enter the Corpus Christi
marathon, bringing their local fan clubs with them. Also, couples from
La Feria, Mercedes, and San Benito, other towns in the Rio Grande
valley, were expected to join. With the valley so well represented, audience members from each town would be rooting for their own couples.
Ross had every reason to expect that his Corpus Christi venture would
be a success.

Ross decided to stage his Corpus Christi dance marathon at the Crystal Beach Park Ballroom. Thanks to Elliott's efforts, the preparations
for opening night were announced in several short articles in the *Texas
South-Press*. The newspaper reported that carpenters were building five
rows of bleachers for 1,500–2,000 people to accommodate the crowds
that were expected. Men's and women's dressing rooms were being
built for the twenty couples who Ross hoped would enter the contest.
Box seats and chairs would circle the 18-by-60-foot arena. Ross sent for

a thousand-dollar loudspeaker system—big money in those days—and had the roof of the ballroom repaired so that the emcee's voice would carry clearly to every corner. He also secured, "at rather high expense," the "red hot" Rio Grande Orchestra.[3] Originally from Indiana, the orchestra had been playing at a resort in the Rio Grande valley when Ross lured them to his marathon.

Ross fed the newspapers a steady stream of details and anecdotes that primed expectations and dictated responses. "Strange things happen during the course of the usual dance marathon," he declared in one article. "During these dances when couples are thrown together day after day for weeks at a time, peculiar things occur, and these happenings are what furnish the main interest to crowds of onlookers."[4] As an example of the "peculiar things," Ross reported that a grandmother who competed in Harlingen won fourth prize and then married her partner. While he cleverly played on the audience's desire to be entertained by the unexpected, he also assuaged their need to know what was going to happen. "As the marathon progresses," he said, "members of the audience will select their favorites. Their applause is the stimulus which keeps the weary contestants at their task during the long hours." He continued:

> With the beginning of this, the greatest endurance marathon dance ever staged in the south, people of the Corpus Christi section will see for the first time one of the most exciting contests yet devised. You have no idea of the excitement one can get out of it. The race is not to the swift here, but to the couple with the most stamina. As the contest continues and the couples begin to fall out, the excitement increases until, in the final days, it works to a fever heat.
>
> There will be a maximum of 20 couples entered. Each will be required to dance 40 minutes of each hour, resting or sleeping the other 20 minutes. The couples are fed eight times a day, usually while dancing. They consume enormous amounts of food—milk, fruit and soup—during the contest.
>
> All will be under care of physicians, trained nurses and physical trainers. Separate training and rest quarters will be furnished for both men and women contestants. Provision will be made to accommodate the thousands who will attend. Every comfort will be provided. Added entertainment will be furnished day and night. The best of orchestras will keep the dancers going day and night.[5]

By the time the marathon opened at 9 p.m. on July 24, 1930, Ross had told his potential audience what to expect, what to look for, what to like. He had created a complete scenario of the forthcoming entertainment.

Buried in his prescriptions for appropriate behavior and responses, and in his constant reassurances about legitimacy, were subtle yet titillating allusions to what might go wrong. He stated that none of the dancers in his shows had ever sustained any injury, then confided that the contestants would be closely monitored during the contest by physicians, nurses, and trainers. The first statement was meant to relieve the anxieties of concerned citizens and authorities, while the second was calculated to attract those interested in witnessing a potentially dangerous spectacle. This double message was all part of his skill as a showman.

Before the opening, Ross was at the ballroom each evening between 9 o'clock and midnight to sign up contestants who wanted to compete for the $1,000 prize money. Anyone could take part—anyone, that is, who was "of good character, of white race, and of more than 18 years of age."[6] For Ross and others who inherited the patriotism of World War I, character, race, and adulthood were the marks of "100 percent Americanism." This racialist, if not racist, imperative, coupled with the segregation of the South, seemed a natural condition of competition to a white veteran. He felt compelled to state it, not because black contestants wanted to compete, but rather to reassure whites about the contest's values. Blacks did come as spectators—Ross was not too proud to take their money—and sat dutifully in the fourth ring, which was assigned to them.

The contestants who were allowed to enter the marathon walked in and saw a whole world under construction. They saw the crude paraphernalia of the contest—the bleachers, the bunting, the oblong dance floor, and the harsh lights. They smelled fresh-cut lumber, heard the sawing and hammering, and were caught up in the commotion of getting ready for the big event.

Ross expected the show to last 420 hours (a little more than two weeks), a "fast show" by Depression-era standards. He liked to set a dramatic and profitable pace during which contestants dropped out quickly. He pushed his marathons by making dancers pick up their feet at all times, rather than allowing them to get by with mere shuffling. Dancers also had to keep moving around the room, which took more energy than idling in one place. Ross also made the rules ever more difficult as the show progressed. For example, rest periods were shortened by a minute each day so that, by the end of the second week, the twenty-minute hourly rest period would be reduced to a mere six minutes.

The ballroom at Crystal Beach was similar to the one depicted in the film *They Shoot Horses, Don't They?* It was built over a pier, suffused with the monotonous sound of waves and sleepy salt breezes. After a few days of dancing, everything could begin to blur. But the master of ceremonies, King Brady, known for his contagious smile and his penchant for keeping dancers in the show, created his own excitement by talking constantly to help keep the dancers alert.

Ross was an expert when it came to setting up the tensions that occurred among the contestants and spectators, and Elliott was an ace at magnifying them in his reports to the local press. Elliott exacerbated the competitive passions between the different towns represented at the Corpus Christi marathon while at the same time giving readers a key to understanding the show by instructing them how to respond should they attend:

> Keen rivalry is developing between Corpus Christi and the valley in the marathon dance at Crystal Beach Park Ballroom, which passed its 172nd hour at 2 o'clock this morning. Of the nine couples remaining on the floor of the 19 who started the search for the $1000 in prizes one week ago last night, four are from Corpus Christi and one is divided.
>
> The valley has given its entries strong support throughout the dance. Harold J. Ross directed a dance at Harlingen before coming to Corpus Christi and the valley residents are marathon educated. They know that it is the applause of the crowds and the donations of various articles or money which keep the contestants going through the killing grind of long hours with practically no sleep.
>
> Corpus Christi fans became awakened last night though and a steady stream of gifts flowed into the arena.[7]

Large-scale tensions, such as the competition between towns, were augmented with small dramas of physical pain and frailty. The world of boxing had taught Ross about the body. He knew that each human body had a story to tell through physical action and physical ailments. The dancers' physical injuries, their causes and cures, were reported and discussed with the same avid interest that sports fans give to the condition of athletes.

Miss White says that when she first felt the pain Saturday night she thought it was a blister in the making. The pain increased and the foot became inflamed.

An attending physician painted her foot with iodine; there was no noticeable break in the skin.

Miss White, although suffering increasing pain, continued to dance for she felt she had more at stake than the other 12 couples because she entered the contest as a challenger.

"I couldn't quit," Miss White said late last night. "Not after saying I'd dance their legs off. I'd rather die first, and we will beat them, too."

The other couples just smile at that and continue dancing.

When the pain became unbearable Miss White asked the physician to cut into the inflamed place and see what was causing the trouble.

A slight incision made late yesterday discovered a sliver of glass a half inch long imbedded in the flesh lengthwise of the foot. Miss White said she couldn't imagine how it got there and apparently it had been there for a long time.

The sliver was removed and Miss White continued in the dance. She and her partner declared they will exceed the winner's dancing hours.[8]

In the same Corpus Christi show, Jackie Wallace's stomach trouble held the interest of the crowd for an entire evening. For two of the dance periods, she was barely able to stand, but at the end of the night Ross announced that he thought she would last several more days.[9] "The hundreds of persons packed into the ballroom enjoyed an evening filled with human interest. The struggle of Jackie Wallace, one of the most popular entries in the dance, to overcome a severe attack of stomach trouble held the interest of the crowd throughout the evening."[10] Creating drama out of the most mundane events made spectators feel that the small occurrences of their own lives mattered.

Proper attention to injuries helped relieve anxiety about the potential cruelty of marathons. It also gave promoters the opportunity to demonstrate their good will even to contestants who were not winners. When Ross noticed red streaks spreading up Myrtle Fultz's leg, evidently a result of a blister on her heel that had become infected, he packed her off to the hospital, regardless of her tears. Fultz had come to Texas with her parents and stayed on after their departure. When she realized that she was broke, she joined the marathon to try to get money to pay her way back home to Montana. After relaying a doctor's report that the inflammation was not serious, but that Fultz would have to stay in the hospital, Ross publicly lamented her condition as he announced his twenty-five-dollar donation toward the price of her ticket home. Ross believed well-cared-for contestants made better performers who attracted larger audiences. What was good for the contestants was, in the main, good for the show and therefore good for the promoter.

The physical condition of the contestants, whether dancing or resting, was of primary importance to Ross. His concern went well beyond showmanship. In a short article, "In the Training Quarters," published in *The Marathoner,* a small informational pamphlet that Ross distributed at his shows, he pointed out: "The contestants, on entering the quarters from a dance period, are instructed how to rest to more complete relaxation by lying flat on the back with limbs and arms straight down, and in this manner the body is permitted quicker and better rest." He also discussed the importance of knowledgeable, impartial physical trainers:

> When the Marathon dance was first started, each team was required to have their own private trainer, but from past experiences this was found to be a great mistake. . . . In several cases it has been known that a private trainer, in order that his team might win, has saturated the pillows of other contestants with chloroform, sprinkled ground glass in the shoes, loaded candy with drugs, etc. So it is the best policy to have reputable head trainers in charge who have nothing personal in the interest of any couple, and nothing but the welfare of his employees at heart. . . . Seldom do these [private] trainers know anything about the human body in so far as rubbing, massaging, etc., and many times unintentionally will do something that causes contestant[s] to drop off the floor.[11]

In his pamphlet Ross documented much of what was wrong with dance marathons. His prescription for curing the problems was the adoption of standardized procedures.

As the number of dancers diminished in Ross's marathons, increasing emphasis was placed on special entertainments. Before the Corpus Christi show opened, the *Texas South-Press* announced a list of entertainments that reads like an anthology of American popular culture of the time: revues, vaudeville shows, a blues singer, the Rio Grande Orchestra, buck-and-wing dancing, and possibly a wedding.[12] Audiences were never simply left to watch tired dancers drag themselves around the stage. Instead, they were constantly treated to a variety of dramas, narratives, sketches, dance routines, guest singers, and orchestras. Ross kept the crowds coming and the dancers moving. He topped it all off with elimination features that brought everything to a timely, climactic, and exciting finish.

Although Ross was definitely cunning and slick, his style and appearance had a certain formality. Solidly built, with slicked-back brown hair, and wearing a sports jacket, tie, and wing-tip shoes, Ross carried himself jauntily. He was easy to spot in a crowd. At the same time, he always kept a cautionary eye on the audience. Very few people knew that he carried pistols under both arms or that he had a metal plate in his head from a war injury.

Ross had a great fondness for Jean Russo, a singer with a deep contralto voice, whom he brought from Chicago to perform in his shows. Russo sang blues and ballads and did impersonations of male dancers and the entertainer Fanny Brice. When she arrived in Texas she was known as "The Little Girl with the Great Big Voice." According to Elliott, Ross had lured her away from her Chicago gangster boyfriend. Ross's guns were, in part, a precaution against the possibility of Jean's former boyfriend showing up to claim her. But Ross was comfortable with weapons from his war days and from his experience in training amateur boxers in Chicago. Ross knew well that quick money generated instant enemies. Although he was always anticipating the appearance of gangsters, a more immediate problem was the metal plate in his head. When he got drunk, his head would throb against the plate and cause such great pain that, according to Elliott, he would go on a rampage.[13]

Ross was a bit of a performer himself. Often, on the dance floor, he played the part of an advocate for both contestants and audience. At the Corpus Christi marathon, when Dick Posey began picking daisies from the air, Ross slapped him several times with a wet towel to bring him back to his senses. On another occasion, during the "girl's cot night," Ross lifted Mary Meyers out of bed when she refused to be awakened. He held her upright, but she collapsed in his arms, almost pulling him across the cot. He tried once more, finally succeeding in getting her to dance for the next forty minutes.

Sometimes Ross played the straight man to his contestants' comic antics. During a "boy's cot night," for example, Roy E. Johnson woke up from his rest period, grabbed Ross, and started dancing him around the floor.[14] Ross went along with these gags, allowing his contestants to subvert his authority just enough to make him seem a likeable guy. He also played the role of the reprimanding parent when he thought contestants were not trying hard enough. When Fay Calloway, the winner of Ross's Harlingen show, seemed indifferent at the Corpus Christi marathon, Ross scolded her publicly for lack of interest in dancing. Ross's accusation reduced Calloway to tears. She said that her partner, Dudley Prade, was the cause of all her troubles. She wanted to dance and put on a show for the crowd, but Prade would not cooperate. This was obviously an instance, Ross concluded, of two persons who do not get along being bound together day after day by the marathon's rules. The audience agreed.[15]

Ross liked putting himself into little scenes at his marathons. He enjoyed appearing as a kind of benign patriarch, even though he, unlike many other promoters, had no paternal nickname, such as Pop, King, or Daddy. As a patriarch Ross presented himself less as an absolute authority than as a man who knew how to control chance. Ross enjoyed one scene in particular because it allowed him to be a gracious facilitator, both for the contestants and the audience. Here is how the *Texas South-Press* reported the event at the Corpus Christi marathon:

Mary and Tommy were dancing around as playfully as two lambs before midnight Thursday. They were doing some serious talking. Tommy was doing most of the arguing. Suddenly she nodded her head in assent, threw her arms around his neck and kissed him.

Then Mary broke away from Tommy and ran toward the rope which bars the way to either dressing rooms or elimination from the dance. The promoter said he rushed to the ropes to meet her thinking she had gone 'haywire' and was quitting. He met her at the ropes and was a mighty surprised man when she hugged and kissed him.

"Tommy and I want to get married, Mr. Ross, can we have the wedding here tomorrow night?"

Ross thought it over a moment and then advised her and Tommy that he didn't want them to be married on a marathon floor, that the church or the home was the place for weddings. But he said they could hold their marriage rehearsal Friday night, if they still were in the dance.

So Friday night about 11 o'clock Mary and Tommy will rehearse their wedding in a mock ceremony to the accompaniment of jazz music from a red hot orchestra. King Brady will be the preacher, Jean Russo will be the maid of honor, Doris Hunt will serve as bridesmaid with Red Spies as the best man.

While the fatal words are being pronounced Miss Russo will sing "The Prisoner's Song." [16]

As Ross staged it, the bride-to-be rushed, not to her father, but to Ross for his consent. He assumed the paternal role and cautioned that lovers should not elope but should be married at church or at home. To this end he played the good, generous father by promising Mary and Tommy a wedding rehearsal on the marathon floor. The rehearsal was to be a mock wedding with 3,000 guests, an orchestra, a wedding cake, a bridal party, and more gifts than could be imagined. Mary would have her "wedding," the audience would be able to attend, and—this is the part he left out of the publicity—Ross would make a bundle.

From this account, it is easy to understand the claim that marathons were nothing more than good, clean fun—and to see that the line between reality and hype was very fuzzy. The mock wedding was one of Ross's favorites. He used it again and again, and audiences loved it. In it both matrimony and marathons were mocked. Less than two months after the Corpus Christi show, when Ross opened a marathon in Galveston, a similar description of a proposal and wedding appeared in a Galveston paper.[17] No doubt Ross and Elliott collaborated on the best way to write up these short dramatic narratives. In both cases, Ross was portrayed as the sponsor of the mock wedding and as the one upholding the sanctity of church and home.

In Corpus Christi, after 755 hours, or thirty-one and a half days, the soon-to-be bride and groom, Mary Meyers and Tommy Thomas, won the first prize of $675, in addition to hundreds of wedding gifts given by spectators. Mary and Tommy had danced from Thursday, July 24, at 9 p.m. until August 24. Other Corpus Christi winners were Doris Hunt and August Spies (second place, $375); Evelyn Jones and Dudley Prade (third place, $150); Jackie Wallace and Roy Johnson (fourth place, $100); and Myrtle Fultz and Ernest Barnard (fifth and last place, $50). Ross had raised the amount of the prize money from $1,000 to $1,350 during the contest, much to the approval of spectators, who had paid to see everything from the opening dance to the closing ceremony. Each of the winning couples was now asked by King Brady to perform part of their specialty act before being awarded their prize money. They did so, to thunderous applause. But the biggest ovation went to the last person to take center stage, Hal J. Ross. The crowds loved him, for he made it all happen.[18] Ross was a local hero of sorts. He had brought the contest to Corpus Christi—and with it fun, passion, entertainment, and temporary jobs.

The lights dimmed, and the crowd left for the last time. Using dollar bills taken in as admission, Ross paid off Ray Dunlap, the business manager, and Elliott. The payoff took place each night in a back room. Their earnings for the entire marathon were $6,000 each. Ross left with what Elliott estimated to be as much as $18,000.[19]

No sooner had the Corpus Christi marathon ended than Ross and his colleagues were on the road to the next town and the next show. Russo had left before the closing ceremony, it was announced, because of a theatrical engagement in New York City. She did not join Ross again until late September when he opened a marathon in Galveston. Between the events in Corpus Christi and Galveston Ross ran a show in an auditorium at a fairground, announcing he would open another in a 10,000-square-foot tent in Laredo. But neither of these marathons was successful for reasons that are not clear. Failures were commonplace in the dance marathon business. Promoters preferred "virgin towns" where people had never seen a dance marathon, but sometimes even virgin towns did not pay off.

Russo was important to Ross. She was an accomplished blues singer with a sizable following, so her name was a draw to the evening shows. Audiences loved the resonance of her contralto voice. And something in the way her plain appearance contrasted with her voice created an air of mystery about her. Her smile was tentative, and her red hair was always ever so slightly out of place, yet she was a poised performer. Russo's image incorporated the tension of an off-key fragility contradicted by a deep and powerful voice.

Russo was also a nice foil to play against the ulterior motives of the men running the show. Ross and King Brady presented Russo as someone who sympathized with the dancers. When a dancer was injured, for example, Russo could be counted on to help pay his or her fare home. Ross liked to describe Russo to his audience as the "mother of all the girls" in the marathon. He frequently placed Russo in charge of any

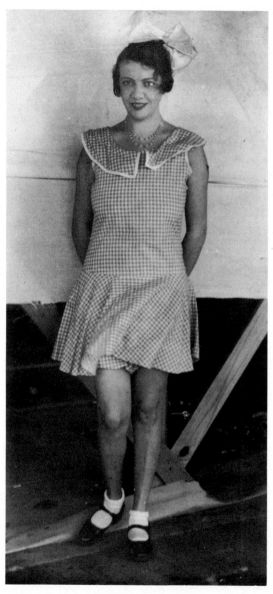

Jane Shannon, "The Little Girl with the Great Big Voice."
(Photo from the scrapbook of Richard Elliott)

"wedding preparations." Together Russo and Ross were able to forge an image of parental concern for the performers and spectators without taking any real responsibility.

At this time Russo was trying to create a new image for herself as a singer. She had outgrown the image of "The Little Girl with the Great Big Voice." Between the Corpus Christi and Galveston marathons she ceased to be Jean Russo and became instead Jane Shannon. Soon after, she began calling herself "Jane Shannon, The Blue Flame of Melody." She owed the new moniker to a contest held in November 1930 on radio station WDAE in Tampa. Listeners were asked to suggest names that summed up the "charms and characteristics of Miss Shannon and her work." Each evening Shannon crooned her songs over the airwaves, including her most popular numbers, "In Old Monterey," "St. Louis Blues," and "I Ain't A-Gonna Cry No More." Three five-dollar turkeys were awarded on consecutive nights to the listeners offering the best suggestions. On the fourth night, still in time for Thanksgiving, she chose the winning name from 400 entries and awarded yet another five-dollar turkey, this one to Charles Luz of 209 Cardy Street.[20] In keeping with the name change, her new image as a performer was sophisticated. The little-girl image really did not suit her matronly body. Certainly it was not compatible with her male impersonation act. "The Blue Flame of Melody," however, conveyed a melancholy passion, a low-burning yet intense glow close to the source of heat. Contradiction governed both these descriptions; she had been a little girl with a big voice, now she was a cool woman with a hot flame.

Shannon alternated radio and club singing with performing for Ross. This worked well for both of them. It added to Shannon's reputation while giving more publicity to Ross's marathons. When Ross opened a marathon at the Cinderella Ballroom in Miami on December 18, 1930, Shannon was featured nightly while also appearing at the Strath Haven Hotel. In addition, she had a three-week engagement at Miami's Alcazar nightclub, along with columnist Walter Winchell, Broadway producer Arch Selwyn, and Miami mayor C. H. Reeder.[21]

Ross and Elliott always tried to win over the local authorities and merchants. Elliott, as the advance man, went ahead of Ross to stake out different towns: "The first thing I did was go around to the city authorities, and not being in show business myself, they would listen to me. I'd tell them it was a square show. We paid the [winning] contestants.

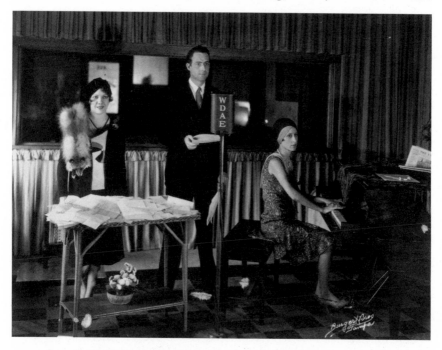

Jane Shannon at station WDAE's contest in which the winning entry
suggested that Shannon be called "The Blue Flame of Melody."
(Photo from the scrapbook of Richard Elliott)

Evidently a lot of people didn't [pay]. I'd make these contacts in
advance."[22]

Galveston, a "virgin town," seemed to be hospitable to the idea of
a marathon, so Elliott wired Ross and they set the opening date for
September 18, 1930. They billed the show as the "Texas Championship" and opened to a crowd of a thousand people watching twenty-
five couples, mostly from Galveston, Houston, and Corpus Christi.
The dancers were competing for $1,000 in prize money. Admission was
twenty-five cents between 5 a.m. and 5 p.m. and fifty cents between
5 p.m. and 5 a.m. The show was broadcast twice daily, from 2 to
2:30 p.m. and from 10 to 10:30 p.m., on KFUL radio. Shannon sang
the blues, and Johnny Maloney was master of ceremonies.

By the time Ross opened his Galveston show, his fifth in Texas,
he was a seasoned promoter. The press reported that he had put on

fourteen other marathons, in Beaumont, Harlingen, and Corpus Christi, Texas; in Mexico City, San Diego, and Denver; and in Hammond, Indiana. The Galveston show followed much the same format as the Corpus Christi show. An 18-by-50-foot dance floor was constructed to accommodate 500 ringside seats. As in Harlingen and Corpus Christi, Elliott was able to get merchants to advertise their affiliation with the marathon. Businesses took out ads in the local papers as Elliott arranged to have their products—soft drinks, milk, bread, steam laundry, hardware, and foot care—advertised at the marathon on large banners hung above the crowd.[23]

The press was enthusiastic about the marathon. Several commentaries were published, apart from Elliott's own reportage. One columnist described it this way:

> Viewed in retrospect, the past week seems to be rather a hazy jumble of events against a background of marathon dancers. . . . It seems amusing the amount of stamina it must take to keep that up. Looks like the participants would never want to dance again. Anyhow, Dick Elliott, the publicity man, formerly of Corpus Christi, solemnly avers that the regular life they are forced to lead leaves them in better physical condition than before they entered. And somebody told us that somebody told them that a doctor had been heard to say that one of the girls, who had been very thin, was actually gaining. Think of that! Anyhow, there is something fascinating about it all.[24]

Another mock wedding was staged in much the same way as at the Corpus Christi marathon. This time Marie McGee of Galveston was the bride. She was given away by Red Long, the floor judge, a man who had served a short prison term as a bootlegger. The groom, W. D. Rogers of Galveston, had as his best man Johnny Maloney, the master of ceremonies. In the ultimate collapse of the boundaries between theater and life, everyone, including the bride and groom, maids and men, judge, emcee, and minister, danced right through the utterance of the fatal "I do."

The Galveston show included other attractions, among them a woman dancing with a sliver of wood in her foot, dancers dropping out, solo contestants finding partners, and rest periods that were first shortened and then cut entirely. There was a ballroom dance exhibition and a Children's Day, during which children under fifteen were admitted

In Galveston, Texas, Hal J. Ross staged a wedding which drew thousands
of spectators. In keeping with the segregation laws of the South,
black spectators were isolated in a special section of the top ring.
(Photo from the scrapbook of Richard Elliott)

for ten cents between 1 and 4 p.m. The Children's Day featured a birthday party, sketches, and the Rio Grande Orchestra. Jane Shannon sang
and displayed charitable sympathy whenever she could.[25] After attending the marathon and hearing Jane Shannon sing "I Ain't A-Gonna Cry
No More," a little Galveston boy became intrigued with the song.
When he had to enter the hospital soon afterward, his mother called the
auditorium and asked Miss Shannon if she would sing the number on
the radio because her little boy wanted to hear it. "So, last night," the
press reported, "Miss Shannon repeated the number assisted by Paul
Jones of the orchestra and Johnny Maloney, master of ceremonies."[26] It
was all new to Galveston, and the local folk loved it. The winners, Billie
and Mac, clocked 755 hours, exactly the same amount of time as for the
Corpus Christi show.

After his marathons in Texas, Ross took a while to get another show going. Elliott went to Kansas City and looked at several towns in the surrounding area where Ross thought he might like to stage a show.[27]

Elliott now had in hand several letters of reference and telegrams as testimonials to the legitimacy and commercial success of Ross's shows. Dr. Charles F. Mares, for example, wrote a letter stating that the human body was capable of amazing endurance. The doctor reported that after examining the contestants at Galveston, he had found no lasting change in pulse rate or heart size, and no pathology. He congratulated Elliott on his nursing staff, the cleanliness of the rest quarters, and the careful manner in which the meals were prepared.[28] Charles Shea, the manager of KFUL radio, wrote a letter stating that the station could successfully bill Ross's marathon as a feature because of the human-interest stories that the performance generated.[29] The editor of the *Galveston Daily News* and the *Galveston Tribune*, E. L. Wall, stated that both papers carried daily stories about the marathon's progress because there was so much reader interest in the event.[30] Last but not least was a copy of a check for $1,000 that had been put up as "earnest money" to pay the contestants in the event that the show was not a success. The cumulative message of these letters and telegrams was that Ross ran a legitimate entertainment that could help other businesses. And, most significantly, even if a Ross marathon should not prove entirely successful, he paid his debts.

Between the middle of October and December 1930 there is no record of Ross's activities. Perhaps he was gambling. He loved the racetrack, where he reportedly lost a fortune.[31] Elliott was on the road scouting for a good town for the next marathon. In November Shannon went to Tampa where she had an engagement singing for WDAE radio, the station that held the contest for her new trade name. There she met radio announcer Jack Negley, who joined Ross's next show as the master of ceremonies.

By December Ross and his crew had settled on Miami as the location of the next marathon. The Miami show was going to be a really big one. Ross had in mind to tour Europe, an enterprise for which he needed a lot of cash. Miami had to be a tremendous success in order for Ross to take on Europe as his next step. So Ross brought three partners in on the deal as investors—Negley, Elliott, and Ray Dunlap. The division of labor was clear. "Dunlap ran the business side of the show, Ross ran the theatrical side of the show, and I ran the public relations," Elliott later explained.[32] Ross leased the Cinderella Ballroom, "Miami's Million Dollar Auditorium," at Northwest Second Avenue and Miami Street. The ballroom had an adjacent parking lot for the numerous Model T automobiles that pulled up. Parking was fifteen cents an hour or twenty-five cents for all day.

Ross wanted more than a reputation for running legitimate shows, he wanted the Miami marathon to be a class act. He hoped to attract both high and low society. Miami was a wild town in 1930. "The Chicago boys were doing great business [in Miami] because there was still prohibition. They used to come to the show every night around midnight with their girlfriends and pack the place," Elliott said.[33] Since he was in their territory, Ross was careful with the gangsters. He knew enough not to end up like Milton Crandall, the promoter of the famous 1928 "Dance Derby of the Century" at Madison Square Garden. Crandall was gunned down by gangsters outside his dance marathon in Chicago in the mid-1930s. Ross and his outfit did experience at least one frightening moment, however, when Dunlap's hotel room was ransacked and several hundred dollars stolen.[34]

The Miami show opened on December 18, 1930. Ross was hoping it would last at least six weeks. On December 22 Ross announced that all the money taken in between 3 and 5 that afternoon would be given to the Greater Miami Christmas Stocking Fund. The *Miami Daily News* headlined the article that announced the benefit, "Marathon Dancers to Aid Miami Needy."[35] On February 2, Ross held another benefit even more indicative of the times. All the proceeds from the evening show were to go to the Mayor's Committee for the Unemployed. The event was part of a series of benefits that Mayor Reeder was putting on at Miami's popular places of amusement to help the unemployed. When Elliott advertised the event as "Aid the Unemployed!" he listed the committee members, along with their official titles. Clearly, they were all prominent citizens: M. S. Altmayer, potentate, Mahi Shrine Temple; Wayne Allen, exalted ruler, B.P.O. Elks; Roger Carter, commander, American Legion; Ellis Hollumus, managing editor, *Miami Herald;* R. A. Reeder, publisher, *Miami Daily News;* and Val C. Cleary, mayor of Miami Beach.[36] Ross and Elliott had cannily courted and won the white power elite of Miami.

The combination of highbrow and lowbrow, of winners and losers, of educated and illiterate, of the established and the marginal was part of

Ross's shows. This mixture was as uniquely American as the entertainments he featured. The question of just how all this would fare in Europe haunted Ross during the winter and early spring of 1931 before his departure in April to Paris. In his Miami show, Ross experimented with the amount and diversity of special entertainments. The marathon included buck-and-wing dancing, tap dancing, waltz exhibitions, yodeling, acrobatic specialties, clowning, comedy skits, guitar playing, singing, and Clarence Schenk and his Rio Grande Orchestra. In addition, there was a fireman's benefit, a bathing beauty contest, girls' and boys' cot nights, a birthday party, a mock wedding, a Christmas party night (including a visit from Santa Claus), a New Year's Eve party, and a theme evening called "A Night in Spain." And, as at all dance marathons, the audience at the evening show danced during the contestants' rest breaks.

The Miami show was tremendously successful. Spectators packed the Cinderella Ballroom. The press avidly followed every aspect of the marathon. The weekly newspaper *Miami Sports* reported that the dance marathon had attracted the largest indoor gathering of any sports event in Miami to date.[37] Along with the article, *Miami Sports* published a handicap list of probable odds to aid those betting on the event. Another newspaper published, under the headline "Brains Needed to Win Dance," an article by one G. E. Bromaghim, a psychology student at the University of Miami. Bromaghim claimed that the fenced-in contestants provided a wonderful opportunity for the study of psychology. The key, he claimed, was in the contestants' dreams, which represented their fears and desires. At the Miami marathon, typical dreams included nightmares about the rope separating the contestants from the rest quarters, dreams about specialty numbers, and dreams about piles and piles of money. The main strain on the dancers, Bromaghim asserted, was not physical but mental. The dancers' physical needs were cared for by a staff of trainers and dieticians, but their minds were dulled by lack of sleep, a condition that reduced their responses to the level of twelve-year-old children. Thus, Bromaghim explained, the winners had to be those with the strongest minds.[38]

The intelligence of Billie and Mac, alias Mr. and Mrs. McGreevy, was never officially measured. Still, they won the Miami show on February 9, 1931, after dancing 1,264 hours—seven and a half weeks. The McGreevys were the same team that had come in second in Cor-

The Cinderella Ballroom in Miami, Florida, where Ross held one of his most successful marathons. (Photo from the scrapbook of Richard Elliott)

pus Christi and first in Galveston. Ross had hired them as his professional contestants. The McGreevys won $700 in prize money, and also the opportunity to sleep for ten hours on Beauty Rest mattresses in a display window at the J. J. Carter Furniture Company. Of course, a crowd of well-wishers crowded around the window to watch them sleep.

After Miami Ross staged another show in Pensacola. The marathon opened on March 31, 1931, and ended on April 5. Ross was becoming nervous about Europe. He wanted extra cash as a cushion before he left. The short Pensacola show was only a moderate success, but it served Ross's purpose. He did not have to invest a lot of money in it, and he made some money out of it. The local American Legion put up half the cost, and in return Ross staged a benefit night to help the Legion build a new home.[39]

Europe was next. The Hal J. Ross party set sail on the *S.S. America* in mid-April. On board were Elliott, Shannon, floor judge Red Long, trainer and floor judge Ernie M. Barnard, Frieda Van Anden, Theodore Isbell, Luman Beede, and a Pensacola contestant, Lois Belle Mark. The

The Cirque Medrano in Paris was the first place where Ross tested the European appetite for American dance marathons. The show was a tremendous success. (Photo from the scrapbook of Richard Elliott)

team stayed in Europe for almost a year as Ross mounted a series of successful shows in France and Germany. When Ross returned in early 1932, he exploited his own desire for class and legitimacy by billing his shows as "European Style Marathons." What characterized these later shows was an elimination feature Ross is credited with inventing, "dynamite sprints." In dynamite sprints contestants raced around the perimeter of the dance floor a set number of times. The last couple to finish was eliminated.[40]

Despite this innovation, Ross soon saw that the marathon business was faltering fast. Ross had dreamed of dance marathons as a new form of entertainment, somewhere between theater and sports, in which rules would govern all aspects of the shows. But fast money drove the marathons. The formats and rules of the shows kept changing so that promoters could garner more cash. Elliott became fed up and decided to try to reenter the newspaper business. He and his wife returned to Topeka, Kansas, then went back to Corpus Christi where Elliott found a job as managing editor of a newspaper. Some of Elliott's friends thought he would not be able to settle down because he had tasted blood money. Once you taste it, the logic went, you can't get it out of your system. In fact, Elliott did become involved in dance marathons again after about a year, when he left Corpus Christi and went to Oregon. "About that time Vernon Balfore put on a show in a town east of Grant's Pass. Helen and I drove down and saw it. . . . Instead of dancing they were holding on to each other and staggering around. Balfore was different from Ross. Ross was straight."[41]

Ross was different, but only up to a point. He wanted to make marathons into a legitimate entertainment. He worked very hard to stage them in an orderly and rule-bound way. Ross was sensitive to issues stemming from America's experience with Prohibition. An unenforceable law, Prohibition spawned bootlegging and gangsterism—a system of behaviors and enforcements with its own logic and hierarchies. Even when Prohibition ended, its underworld heritage continued, blurring the boundaries between legitimate business and criminal activity. Coming from the marginal world of professional boxing, Ross was all too aware of the slippery boundaries between what was acceptable and respectable and what was despised yet more or less publicly practiced. Ross saw that boxing, even with all its connections to the criminal underworld, survived because it was rule-governed. He wanted to achieve the same recognition and governance for dance marathons.

After returning from Europe, Ross returned to Mexico City, San Diego, Denver, and Hammond, Indiana, to stage his European-style marathon. He was always regarded as a legitimate and more or less honest promoter. He continued to introduce new ideas to make his shows more entertaining. He never gave up on his dream of making dance marathons into an American sport. But Ross's post-European successes never matched his Miami show. Marathons themselves were in decline, and even a promoter of Ross's energy could not salvage them. Sometime in the 1930s, I cannot determine exactly when, Ross stopped staging marathons. What happened to him next is not clear. There is a rumor that he lost every dollar at the races. After that, according to Elliott, he worked as a hired hand in a track stable, close to the nags he loved so much, until one day he was fatally kicked in the head by a horse.

$\mathcal{S}ix$

The National Endurance
Amusement Association

Few reliable promoters with whom I was connected
during my brief sojourn in the walkathon field impressed
me as the type of men that are far-sighted enough to take
their endeavors and investments out of the shaky, pre-
carious class of a "racket" and, by following the plan
suggested by Kaplan and *The Billboard,* lead it into the
soundly entrenched niche of the much-needed public
mass entertainment field that it should and can and
maybe will occupy.

Ward Keith, "Uplift Field of Endurance Entertainment,"
Billboard, 15 December 1934

$\mathcal{I}$n April 1934 Jimmy Scott, a ballroom dancer who had danced in
the "Dance Derby of the Century" at Madison Square Garden in
1928, published an article in *Billboard* questioning how long dance
marathons as a genre would last. Scott was the first to put forward concerns that had long been troubling promoters. His article provoked a
public debate about creating an organization to regulate marathons.
Scott's article and those that followed exposed the ills of the business
and seriously considered the possibility of an antidote in the form of a
professional organization. *Billboard* became the medium of the debate
and the advocate of the newly formed organization, the National Endurance Amusement Association (NEAA). The articles were coinci-
dental with the beginning of the strongest legislative drive to ban dance
marathons.

Scott's concern that marathons would soon die out centered on inexperienced promoters who were ruining the potential of marathons to become a legitimate form of entertainment.[1] To dramatize his point he depicted what he considered a typical scenario:

> Looking in on a going show or two, observing an enthusiastic audience and a line at the box office, with seats sold and, when vacated, resold, Mr. Green promoter is all set to reap a harvest—of headaches! Lacking even a fraction of the knowledge and experience along with financial backing of the successful producer in the field, he rents a hall and induces a group of boys and girls—mostly inexperienced and unprepared—to enter. Because of a small bankroll he engages a staff, from emcee all down the line, with lowest salary as the principal qualification. Inefficiency causes trouble to start probably with the first of seven or eight daily meals. Before long the kids on the floor, sensing that all is not kosher, become unmanageable. Patrons lose interest in the thing, if it attracted any in the first place. Result: No prize money and kids stranded, help unpaid, causing agitation toward unfavorable legislation. The story of the "Flopathon" is all too familiar to some of us. Reputable producers have had flops too. But invariably they have paid prize money, salaries to help and all other obligations, thereby promoting confidence in their future shows.[2]

Billboard was the logical place for commentary such as Scott's to be aired. As a major trade journal devoted to the popular entertainment industry, *Billboard* featured articles portraying different facets of the marathon business. It also ran advertisements for and announcements of upcoming shows. Beginning in January 1934, ads requesting marathon contestants ran regularly on the "Feature News" page. By February of the same year, a short column appeared under the heading "Endurance Shows" with the subtitle "Danceathons—Walkathons—Speedathons." Writer Don King assembled the column, based on information sent from publicists for marathon promoters around the country. The section quickly grew to one and then two pages, with a special section titled "Endurance Notes" where marathoners could contact one another, making both business and personal announcements without charge.

In his article, Scott portrayed marathons as a business requiring special knowledge, experience, and expertise. However true this might have been, it did not affect the increasing number of local ordinances that banned marathons. Only transforming marathons into a well-regulated, legitimate entertainment could counter the ordinances. Inexperienced promoters were not the only problem. Even reputable promoters were known for staging marathons that milked the audience for weeks beyond their logical limits, making it tough to sell a second show in that locality. Even contestants turned the events to their own ends. "Hotel dancers," as they were pejoratively called, soaked up funds for room and board (hence the name) before the marathon began and then skipped town before the contest opened to look for another free deal. Remedies for these troubles would not be easy to concoct.[3]

Two months passed before another article continued the debate that Scott had begun. "Why a Successful Walkathon—Marathon?" by Eddie Gilmartin rehashed what Scott had said. Clearly, the debate was still current even though it had not progressed very far. The issues were common knowledge to those in the business. "Now that marathons and walkathons have passed the craze stage inasmuch as there is very little or no virgin territory," Gilmartin began, "the great question is: What is going to come of it? Will it die or will it be accepted as an American institution, or as an entertaining and popular form of divertissement in the amusement realm?" Gilmartin, who identified himself as a manager, floor judge, and radio master of ceremonies, cautioned auditorium and park managers about inexperienced promoters. "Many ex-employees think they know it all, but there are too many angles and connections that combine to make a good show." The relationship of these "angles and connections" to the future of the business was what everyone was trying to figure out.[4]

Promoter Hal J. Ross soon joined Scott and Gilmartin in the debate about marathons, taking the approach that marathons were good, clean entertainment. Addressing an article titled "The Poor Man's Night Club," which had appeared in *Esquire* the previous year, Ross asserted that marathons were now "properly the family man's night club, so conducted that a man can take his whole family and get a lot of laughs and thrills for a nominal fee."[5] The *Esquire* article had depicted marathons as events that placed the cruelties of life on display for the down and out, who were thereby assured that somebody else had it worse than they. But Ross was convinced that the entertainment value of marathons went beyond the circumstances of the Depression.

These two points of view were not simply the result of different interpretations; they were also evidence of the range of shows that were being presented. Different promoters put on different kinds of shows, making marathons not only hard to characterize, but also difficult to regulate. Some were good, clean fun; others stressed the plight of the contestants and exploited sadomasochistic themes; still others featured off-color, downright lewd humor imported from burlesque. In addition to the rules, the entertainments and the atmosphere of marathons, their muscle and style—the things that held them together and made them entertaining—varied greatly.

Ross thought that if the marathon business got rid of its "racketeers, chiselers, and novices," the future was promising. Ross did not name names, nor did any of the other writers who entered the debate in *Billboard*. He advised contestants to compile scrapbooks of programs as proof of their participation to differentiate themselves from "hotel dancers." He also devised a way for them to make sure the prize money would be awarded if they won the contest. Contestants were to demand an ironclad guarantee from the promoter that the prize money would be awarded no matter what the circumstances. To this end, contracts could be drawn up between promoters and contestants. Contestants could also insist that promoters deposit 10 percent of the gross receipts of the previous day's business in a local bank every morning until the total amount of the prize money advertised was reached. This way the prize money, placed in a separate account in the name of "The Walkathon Contestants' Prize Money," would remain safe.[6]

Contracts made business deals legitimate. And legitimacy—as a business and an entertainment—was what Ross and some other promoters wanted. Thus it was just a matter of time before an attorney entered the field. Richard S. Kaplan had been around marathons in Indianapolis and Chicago. He enjoyed the sport, and the legal questions relating to endurance shows intrigued him. Unlike Ross, who liked to advise contestants, Kaplan directed most of his recommendations to the promoters. According to Kaplan's first *Billboard* article, in October 1934, there were ten important points for promoters to keep in mind when drawing up a contract.

1. The contract should contain a clause expressly setting forth that in the event a contestant voluntarily leaves the walkathon within a

period of eight days, without being disqualified, his trunk or other possessions shall remain in the custody of the promoter as liquidated damages, or in lieu thereof the contestant shall pay the promoter for the cost of feeding and sheltering the contestant before the contest started and during his stay.

This will eliminate the "hotel marathoners" who flitter and flutter from one place to another sponging off this and that promoter.

2. Set out definitely the prize or prizes to be offered, whether or not the prize had been set aside and placed in trust for the winners or if the prize shall be set aside out of the gross profits or earnings and, if the latter, what percentage of the gross shall be so set aside.

3. How many hours shall the contest run before it shall be called a contest?

4. Under what conditions may the promoter close the contest and/or refuse to pay prize money?

5. In the event the show runs more than the stipulated number of hours necessary to be termed a contest and same is closed by law or otherwise outside of the power of the promoter, what shall be done with the prize money in trust or set aside out of the gross?

6. Set out definitely your responsibility with reference to illness or accidents occurring to a contestant during the course of the contest.

7. How old shall a contestant be before he may enter and what penalty if any shall be attached if false statements shall have been made by the contestant in entering the contest and such false statement is later discovered during the contest's run?

8. Be sure to set out the authority possessed by the judge and trainer and what penalties attach to a failure on the part of the contestant to obey orders of such judge or trainer.

9. Be sure to stress the point that the promoter shall have the right to change the rules governing the show at any time during the run of the contest. (You'll find this clause a very valuable one.)

10. Be sure to stress the fact that you are *not* responsible for the loss of money or personal effects left in quarters. Such money should be left in the box office of the show and a receipt given to the contestant, while the personal effects must be carefully watched by the contestant. (There have been several suits brought by contestants lately around this question, so be careful on this point.)[7]

In giving advice, Kaplan used the civic and contractual language of law, with no trace of mockery or subversion. Use of such language for a popular subculture event reveals his explicit alignment with authority.

Kaplan clearly did not comprehend that resistance against authority was part of the narrative and performance texts of marathons. While his advice about drawing up contracts was sympathetic to the problems promoters encountered, it also had an officious tone that was alien to marathons as a genre.

This was the first of many articles that Kaplan wrote for *Billboard.* The publication's editorials fully endorsed the efforts of Kaplan and others to make marathons into a legitimate business. In the editorial following Kaplan's first article, King invited further discussion from promoters and contestants. Soon after that Kaplan proposed that *Billboard* become the official vehicle for the dissemination of information, with promoters and contestants using it for "propaganda" and education.[8]

Kaplan stressed that education was the answer to widespread misconceptions about the shows. From a case he had defended involving the closing of a walkathon, Kaplan provided the following exchange he had had with a witness for the prosecution:

Q. Have you ever witnessed a walkathon?
A. No—and I don't want to see one.
Q. Why don't you want to see one?
A. Oh, they're cruel—and—and terrible.
Q. If you have never been to a walkathon how do you know they are cruel and terrible?
A. Well, I've heard a lot about them.
Q. Do you approve of prize fights?
A. Certainly, they're okay. Everyone sees them. It's sport.
Q. Do you mean to say that a prize fight, which endangers the life of every participant, is okay, while a walkathon, which had never caused the death of a single participant or the serious injury of such a participant, is cruel?
A. Oh, I never knew that. But I still think it's terrible.[9]

Kaplan carefully exposed the witness's prejudices, but he did not yet accurately recognize their origin. Uneducated popular opinion about marathons hardly accounted for the bad reputation of the events. Kaplan was just beginning to get a sense of who the opposition really was. Alluding to this, he cautioned: "The reputable operators in the endurance field almost daily encounter evidence that certain interests are making a well-planned effort to eliminate endurance contests from the amusement horizon. There are ample ways available to encourage and foster legislation in the form of state laws and city ordinances to either prohibit this type of entertainment entirely or place such excessive taxes and license fees in effect that they automatically gain their end."[10]

The real opposition was the burgeoning motion picture chains. These were the "certain interests" pressing city councils into passing laws to prohibit endurance shows of any kind.[11] Promoter Leo Seltzer claimed that many of the laws governing endurance shows had been put on the books in the initial phase of nonstop dancing in 1923.[12] These draconian measures, Seltzer said, were the basis for future laws governing endurance shows in the 1930s. In fact, both Kaplan and Seltzer were correct. Many laws were put on the books in the early 1920s, but many more were added in the 1930s.

Scott, Gilmartin, Kaplan, and Seltzer all credited the popularity of dance marathons to legitimate promoters who were able to stage successful shows. All agreed that the shows were threatened by "hotel dancers," novice and fly-by-night promoters, inexperienced contestants, and the movie industry. In a series of articles they turned their warnings into prescriptions for successful shows. These suggestions ranged from an efficient kitchen staff, proper sanitation system, and linen supply, to a good emcee with "air" at least twice a day, professional contestants, extra entertainment features, and a good, clean atmosphere. At the end of each of these articles, the authors proposed organizing dance marathons. No one knew exactly how to go about it yet, but they gradually worked it out in the pages of *Billboard* over the following months.

By the end of December, some positive responses to the pleas for organization had been published in "Forum," a special section of *Billboard*. The favorable responses provided the impetus for the next step. The time had come for an official meeting, to be held January 28, 1935, at the Sherman Hotel in Chicago. All promoters were urged to participate. A convention reservation form, which was also a pledge to attend the event "in the spirit of open mindedness and with a willingness to cooperate," was printed in *Billboard*.[13] Participants were instructed to fill out the form and send it to *Billboard* in care of Don King.

The response to the proposed convention was poor. Another editorial, titled "Stalling," appeared in *Billboard*, followed by another convention reservation form. No one was accusing any particular promoter of stalling, the editorial said, but as of the date when the current issue went to press, the magazine had received only three or four reservation forms. The convention was just sixteen days away. Because there were factions with much ill feeling among them, there was concern that the field would not be accurately represented. "To attempt a meeting without such representation would be silly and a waste of time and money."[14]

Promoters felt threatened by the prospect of this meeting, beyond the possible awkwardness of facing their competitors. Some may have feared that they would lose their independence and become beholden to an organization whose rules they did not care to follow. Others were perhaps worried about having to contribute large sums of money to the organization. Kaplan and King were considering a way of funding the organization that would cut into promoters' profits. "Whatever it is that is decided may be needed for the operation of an association will, you may be sure, be proportioned in some equitable way that will tax you no more than a small percentage on each ticket sold at your window," assured *Billboard*.[15]

The attempt to organize was in keeping with the tenor of the times. The business community had been organizing management. Organized labor was in the midst of expansion. Organized management held more power over labor, but it faced hundreds of strikes by unionized laborers newly aware of their own power.[16] Some promoters must have felt that although an organization might serve them well, it could also be a signal for their employees to demand better working conditions and higher wages. For dancers and other marathon employees to organize would challenge the fragile balance of power.

Unity was the express purpose of the proposed organization, but the articles and editorials in *Billboard* stressed individual benefit as the desired result. Promoters felt that they had been successful because of the unique variations they had incorporated into their own shows. Moreover, they all had different ways of making financial arrangements with local businesses and of handling cash flow. Endurance dance promoters had free rein over their enterprises, and understandably they hesitated to endorse measures that might curtail their entrepreneurial freedom.

The attempt to organize required nonpartisan leadership. There was some suggestion that representatives from *Billboard* become the official governing body of an endurance show organization. *Billboard* had served the business well thus far, so why not make its role official?

By January 19 the response to the convention had improved. Several key promoters had sent in their reservation forms and consented to have their names published in *Billboard*. The key respondents were Charles F. Noltimier, Hal J. Ross, Guy H. Swartz, J. B. Steinel, George W. Pughe (by proxy), Hugh Talbott, S. M. Fox and his partner Louis Slusky, Leo A. Seltzer, Carl W. Raabe, Ray C. Alvis and his partners Harry Fitzpatrick and Harry G. Newman, Red Leinen, and attorney Richard S. Kaplan.[17] Taken together, these promoters well represented the field and accounted for the majority of leading names in the business. This was the turning point, *Billboard* concluded, and more names were expected to pour in now that the ice had been broken.

But the next week saw the addition of only two more names: Harry H. Cowl and Fred Crockett. Still, the editorial was upbeat, stressing that at the very least, the convention would be an interesting encounter. At most, however, if prominent promoters could resolve their differences, the future of dance marathons might take a new direction. After twelve years and three phases of existence, dance marathons might now become a legitimate form of American entertainment, with status equivalent to that accorded professional wrestling, boxing, and the circus.

On a cold, windy Monday morning in Chicago, the promoters of endurance shows began their meetings. The delegates proceeded in an orderly fashion. The first item of business was to appoint a Ways and Means Committee, which consisted of King, Swartz, Kaplan, Seltzer, and Noltimier, with Len Ivey as secretary.[18] The committee then selected King, who was considered to be independent from the business, as the chair. King explained that each promoter present was to have one vote on each issue. He went on to offer a definition of *promoter*, so that all present would be in consensus about voting power. A promoter was anyone who was currently operating or had operated an endurance contest. Those voting at the meeting were Raabe, Seltzer, Pughe, Talbott, Ross, Ray Dunlap, Noltimier, Swartz, Pat Webster, Ed Buere, Leinen, and Mrs. Ben C. Kubby. This group was significantly different from those who were listed in *Billboard* as pledging attendance. Steinel, Fox, Slusky, Alvis, Fitzpatrick, Newman, Cowl, and Crockett were missing, while Webster, Buere, Raabe, and Mrs. Kubby were newly added. Out of the original seventeen promoters who pledged their attendance, only eight had shown up. With the additional four promoters, this made twelve voters. King and Kaplan were present, but they abstained from voting because they were not promoters.

Next Seltzer proposed that only promoters be admitted into the organization. Kaplan suggested that contestants and other employees be included also so that they would be covered by the charter drawn at the meeting. This agreed on, every worker in the field could be part of the new organization.

The rest of the three-day meeting was devoted to defining the purpose of the National Endurance Amusement Association and to developing a charter that covered every aspect of the business. The association pledged to provide:

1. A service which will provide the operator with legal advice free at all times when the matter involved concerns the operator's show.

2. Free contracts for all operators, such contracts to be uniform. As for example, a uniform contract between operator and contestant, uniform leases, options and all forms of agreement between the operator and the public.

3. A fight against unfavorable legislation. Model regulatory plans and measures to be prepared and presented to legislatures for adoption and passage, thus anticipating and offsetting possible prohibitory legislation.

4. To do everything in its power to eliminate the irresponsible operator.

5. To carry on a continuous campaign of education of the general public and public officials, and by means of pamphlets, newspaper publicity, letters, broadcasts, etc., setting forth the great amusement possibilities of the Endurance Show as operated and practiced by members of the association. The thought being that contestants, staff people and the public in general will become educated to the point where they will give preference to shows conducted by members of the association when answering and responding to advertisements.

Legal advice, free contracts, model regulatory plans, elimination of irresponsible promoters, and promotion of the NEAA were to be the special advantages of membership. Where the tone of the charter was adversarial, the opponent was clearly identified as irresponsible promoters. If the charter could be implemented, the entire field might change its face. By the close of the meeting, the tone was ecstatic. It appeared that endurance contests had a chance of becoming legitimate entertainments.

Billboard devoted two pages to the conference. Under the blaring headline, "Organization a Reality," it gave a summary of the meeting, followed by extensive excerpts from the Code of Fair Practice that had been proposed by Kaplan and amended by the promoters. The code addressed all the situations that might occur in connection with endurance entertainment. These fell under the following headings: "Definition of Endurance Contest, Contracts, Prize Money, Ages of Contestants and Employees, Publicity and Publications, Facilities and Sanitation, Contestants—Disqualification, Medical and Surgical Care, Acceptance of Contestants, Sub-Executives—Types to be Used, Conduct of Contests—Use of Implements on Floor, Physicians—Authority, and Legal Bureau."

The code was far-reaching in its attempt to provide guidelines for the business. Contestants were to receive free medical, surgical, and dental care for the duration of the contest. Physicians would have the final authority to determine whether a contestant was fit to enter or continue in the competition. Prize money would be deposited in a bank before the contest began and could be withdrawn only with the consent of the winning contestants. Promoters were not to use chains or straps to tie contestants together for special elimination features or for any other reason, as had sometimes been done.

Promoters had to take legal age into consideration when hiring contestants and employees. They were to follow the health codes of any given city and provide suitable, sanitary rest quarters. Promoters now had the right to confiscate the personal belongings of any contestant who left the premises of the contest without permission and retain the items until the contestant reimbursed the promoter for any expenses incurred in relation to the contestant. In the event that a promoter decided not to use a contestant, the promoter was required to pay for the contestant to return to his or her place of origin. All promoters now had to use uniform contracts in the employment of contestants. Read one way, the code provided a plan to secure the operations of endurance shows; read another way, it was a documentation of the problems that had made the NEAA necessary.

The NEAA had taken hold of the field for the moment. Soon key promoters—Fox, Noltimier, Talbott, Pughe, and Ross—began to announce their shows in *Billboard* using the NEAA insignia. Members set themselves apart by pointing to the code of ethics that governed their shows.

An N.E.A.A. floor judge checking to see if the contestant's knee is touching the floor. (Photo from the scrapbook of Richard Elliott)

A month after the convention, "legitimate" promoters, or promoters who wished to become legitimate, were still being urged to join. All that was required was an initiation fee of $100. Joining the NEAA was put forward as the only antidote to the increasing nationwide opposition to marathons.

On February 22, 1934, Indiana banned endurance contests, and Kansas was about to pass similar legislation. Kaplan wrote an urgent editorial in *Billboard* asking promoters to join NEAA to help fight the "theatrical organizations" behind the ministerial associations that were protesting the shows. This was the first time that Kaplan had spelled out some of the legal strategies he was developing. In May or June, he said, after the new law in Indiana went into effect, the association, in collaboration with Talbott, would challenge it by opening a show. After Indiana, the NEAA would contest the laws of Iowa, Maine, New Hampshire, Virginia, Texas, New York, and "every city and town enforcing anti-Endurance show legislation." The NEAA was also planning to send out model ordinances and statutes to city councils and legislatures. This would take a great deal of court action, effort, and money. Kaplan hoped to prove the ordinances unconstitutional.[19]

Kaplan's editorial shifted the organization's focus from illegitimate promoters to the legal battles it would have to fight in order for the marathon business to stay alive. The marathon business faced three main problems: illegitimate promoters were giving the shows a bad name; labor was not governed by any organizational rules; and legislation banning dance marathons was increasing.

Historically most American workers had realized they could gain bargaining power by banding together and negotiating as a group, but individual marathon dancers took no such action.[20] As a result, they could not deprive employers of their labor by striking, and they could not force promoters to make concessions.

Officially, dancers were contestants, not employees; dance marathons were contests, not jobs. But dance marathons were only contests in appearance. In actuality, they were planned entertainments employing regular entertainers who moved from show to show. Some of these entertainers enjoyed considerable bargaining power for themselves because they were sought by promoters who wanted their special skills. Those who considered themselves professional marathoners were able to make private deals negotiating their employment. (Contestants who did not make these private deals still received "pay" in the form of food and lodging and whatever money the crowds sprayed onto the dance floor.) This situation was to the advantage of both the talented marathoner and the promoter. The marathoners got the extra money or even the salary they sought, and the promoters got the entertainment crucial to their shows without having to pay everyone fairly.

The division between professional and amateur contestants divided the marathon work force into two factions. Here is a typical scenario from the point of view of one amateur contestant, Edna Smith, who took part in a 1928 marathon in Harlem:

> The only tension [at the marathon] was about the Puerto Rican couple. The little Puerto Rican girl was very beautiful and down the line somewhere the manager decided the couple would get married on the floor. The idea was we could keep dancing. It would be a dancing wedding. When the deal went down it came out they were already married, that's when some of the contestants got upset. Someone said they were already married and they were just out to get

more money and it wasn't fair. But they were beautiful dancers. Sometimes stage stars would come in and ask to see ballroom dancing, and the Puerto Rican couple got all the money. No one else was ever able to do that. They could do some beautiful things. They used to pull all the money down from the audience. The rest of us just kind of had to shuffle around.[21]

The Puerto Rican couple knew the promoter and had danced for him previously. Predictably, they were among the last three couples on the floor when the contest closed.[22] The amateurs protested the preferential treatment of the professionals; they prevented the mock wedding from happening. But they could not stop the talented couple from being favored by the spectators or from holding out until the contest was over. In fact, it was to everyone's advantage to have a popular draw like the Puerto Rican couple. But in the long run, situations like these alienated amateur contestants. In some cases, amateurs turned against the shows entirely.

It was typical for the grievance about the wedding to be brought to management instead of to the Puerto Rican couple themselves. Management and labor were opposed, but labor was also divided against itself. This further division, a consequence of the varying abilities and professional status of the contestants, served the interests of management. Both amateurs and professionals brought their complaints to the promoters, who were then able to negotiate in their own self-interest. If a promoter was clever enough, he could make both amateurs and professionals believe they were being served.

Many professionals, however, eventually recognized that they were being exploited. Norma Jasper commented that she and her close friend and fellow contestant Faye DeMarco were "alike in the respect that we never told people we were marathoners. In retrospect we both felt exploited. Although, at the time, we were making money, and having a great time."[23] This imbalance of power in favor of management, of course, was exacerbated by the high unemployment of the 1930s.

Marathon employees during this time were not eager to challenge promoters. There was resentment, but it remained on the individual level. For one thing, it was hard to mobilize in a work setting that was founded on competition. Dance marathoners embraced competition, even coercive competition, as a necessary tactic for a contestant to "make it." An unjust social order based on survival of the fittest was part of the show. Even if a marathon was entirely orchestrated down to the winning couple, the narrative it presented to the public was one of inequality determined by struggle. In the eyes of spectators, this made the winners doubly triumphant. At the same time, many of the contestants were friends. Their apparent "competition" was part of the act. Even though contestants like Jasper and DeMarco may have had "a great time," they were also disillusioned, not only with what winning meant, but with how the system worked. The same was true for those who wanted to use marathons as a stepping stone to become professional entertainers. Disappointment was not enough to surmount competition and unite contestants into taking action on their collective behalf. Even if such action had begun to stir at a show, it would have had limited time to develop. Marathons, after all, were designed to eliminate people, and many contestants participated only once.

Although contestants were included in the NEAA, the real plea for membership always was made to promoters. Promoters controlled the organization's finances. Of course, they also created most of the situations that jeopardized the endurance field. Kaplan, who seemed to be undaunted by his apparent lack of success at getting promoters to join the NEAA, continued to write editorials for *Billboard* with a "join the bandwagon" tone. "Operators Need NEAA" was the headline for his March article, which claimed that the ranks were swelling but that more members were needed. Moreover, Kaplan said, the organization had already solved several problems for its members. Two promoters had been in a dispute over money; another promoter had been prevented by the police from opening his show; still another had discovered that some of his contestants, who were on the floor, had received telegrams asking them to join different shows. In each case, the NEAA stepped in to resolve the problem.[24]

Kaplan claimed that movie theater managers were using their association (he did not name it) to wipe out dance marathons. As usual, he cited no evidence. It is doubtful that Kaplan made assertions like these simply to incite promoters to action. In retrospect, it seems clear that the accusation—which may well have been true—did serve a particular purpose. It gave a face to what previously had been a powerful but anonymous enemy.

Kaplan emphasized that only an organization like NEAA could battle the prohibitory legislation that was rapidly making marathons a thing of the past. He invoked the changes that were sweeping the country by arguing that there could be a "New Deal" for the legitimate operator. He summed up his plea by singling out movie theater owners and managers as the opposition, probably making them seem more organized than they actually were. "The fight for existence is on. Will the theater owners and managers drive you from the field or are you going to fight? Only by joining the National Endurance Amusement Association can the answer be affirmatively made."[25]

At the end of March, promoter Ernie Mesle's dance marathon scored a victory in Dedham, Massachusetts, just outside the Boston city limits. Although the show had a permit issued by the town, "certain organizations" were loudly criticizing the show. Mesle brought his case not to court, but to the people of Dedham. At a town meeting, covered in local and Boston newspapers, the vote was 169 to 30 in favor of the show.[26] But this coup seems to have been achieved without the NEAA.

Kaplan, meanwhile, was busy in California dealing with another threat. Three top promoters and members of NEAA, Hayden, Ross, and Pughe, were encountering "special interest" opposition pushed by prominent local attorneys. Ross and Hayden wanted to open in San Francisco and Pughe in Santa Clara. In the process of opening, Pughe was arrested for violating an old ordinance prohibiting marathons. Kaplan got Pughe out of jail and obtained a restraining order permitting his show to go on.[27] Because movie theater interests were strongest in California, this was hailed as a major step in securing dance marathons' right to exist. Shortly thereafter, Kaplan claimed that he had definite proof that "motion picture interests" were organizing to promote legislation against dance marathons.[28]

The many editorials and pleas for action printed in *Billboard* subtly shifted from problems within the business to problems pressing from the outside. Infighting and irreconcilable differences among promoters had kept the NEAA from developing regulations that would turn marathons into a "legitimate" business. Now various movie theater associations were increasingly pushing for legislation to ban marathons on the grounds that the shows were unregulated.

By October 5, 1935, twenty-four states were enforcing statutes against endurance contests. On that same date there appeared in *Billboard* a sad letter from contestant Stew Allen, summing up the fate of the NEAA with a series of questions. "Many well-known gentlemen who have made their living by the endurance game sent telegrams saying they would support the NEAA, but when money was needed why did so many back away? Those mentioned were willing to do all they could to help fight for their bread and butter. Others promised to go along but they dropped out of the picture. Where are all the NEAA insignias? . . . Why are there so few [endurance] ads in *Billboard?*" [29]

The second meeting of the NEAA—the last large-scale attempt to unite the business—took place May 27–29, 1936, at the Sherman Hotel in Chicago. The endurance-show pages of *Billboard* were filled with the same pleas urging promoters and others who wanted to save the business to attend. But by May 25 only fifteen men, including Kaplan and King, had registered. Regulation was again the subject, but the focus this time was on the masters of ceremonies, floor judges, trainers, nurses, and contestants. Promoters had included employees in the codes established at the first meeting; now they were urging contestants to join, promising that the NEAA would answer their needs.

> Membership in the NEAA will provide the contestants and employees with numerous benefits, among them being (1) Protection against operators who do not pay prize money or wages, thus eventually eliminating illegitimate operators; (2) Guarantee suitable working conditions for employees; (3) Provide transportation for contestants who have walked more than 500 hours and who have been regularly disqualified; (4) Protect both contestants and employees against abuse of powers by operators; (5) Protect the legitimate contestant against chiseling and conniving illegitimate operators and contestants; (6) Arbitrate disputes which may arise between contestants, employees and operators and in every way endeavor to raise the standard of the endurance show and aid in advancing the interests of those who make up this important form of entertainment. [30]

As good as this sounded, it was nothing new. All these points had been covered in the NEAA charter devised at the first meeting. What then were the conveners in Chicago trying to accomplish? Perhaps Kaplan and the others thought that because the number of employees far exceeded the number of promoters, their membership would give NEAA the strength of numbers it needed. Or perhaps, faced with low attendance at the meeting, and in lieu of making a new attack on the old problem they still faced, the members of NEAA could only restate blandly their desire for increased membership. As an earlier *Billboard* headline had noted, organization was a reality with the formation of the NEAA, but it did not make any difference. Promoters and contestants were just not joining.

Despite all the articles in *Billboard* describing the efforts to organize, for many of those in the business the NEAA was just another marathon scam. Dancer Stan West saw the NEAA as just a figure of speech that was used when closing a show. He never considered joining the organization. "It never did materialize to any extent, and was used as another caption, to keep the public informed that a new judge was brought in, the last week or so of the show to form its conclusion by executing tight elimination features." [31]

The NEAA slipped out of dance marathons as rapidly as it had arrived. But even without the NEAA, the shows went on. Lawyer Kaplan continued to keep his vigil, creating in *Billboard*'s ever smaller endurance-show section a new column where he freely offered his legal advice to all concerned.

Seven

UNNEGOTIABLE REALITIES

A broken hearted mother today awaited the arrival of
her daughter's body on a train leaving late last night
after almost a week of desperate efforts on the part of
friends here to raise funds that would save the girl from
a pauper's grave. The mother wired enough money to
make up the needed sum. The story of a girl who danced
her life away was revealed in grim tragedy today at City
Hospital where the body has lain unclaimed since Sunday.
Death was due to a form of meningitis; physicians at the
City Hospital today indicated that the fatality was probably due to over strain from marathon dancing.

American Social Hygiene Association,
report, 24 April 1934

The legal obstacles against dance marathons were clearly increasing. Prompted by disturbing news reports about dance marathons,
Bascom Johnson, in charge of legal and protective measures at
the American Social Hygiene Association, on February 24, 1934, sent
a letter of inquiry to chiefs of police in all forty-eight states.[1] In it
he asked for information concerning laws regulating or prohibiting
dance marathons or walkathons. By May he had received replies from
Birmingham; Los Angeles; Oakland; Denver; Atlanta; Boston; Somerville, Massachusetts; Minneapolis; Atlantic City; Fargo, North Dakota; Providence; Seattle; Milwaukee; and Cheyenne, Wyoming (see
appendix for legislation). In 1933 or 1934 the majority of these cities had
passed ordinances banning dance marathons. Birmingham was the exception, having enacted its ordinance banning endurance contests as
early as 1930.

Newark was the only city responding to Johnson that did not have an antimarathon ordinance. The Newark police chief explained that anyone wishing to stage a marathon in Newark had to apply for permission from his office. The captain of the precinct where the marathon was going to be held had to investigate the proposed building and its facilities, the neighborhood in which the marathon was to take place, and the possible moral effect it would have. After the captain's report was received, the chief of police took up the matter with the local director of public safety before a final decision was made. At the end of his letter, the chief stated that he was not in sympathy with marathon dances or walkathons, because he believed they did not "serve to further the wholesome spirit of recreation for which they are intended."[2]

The response of the Newark police chief was the most sympathetic that Johnson received. He was the only responding official willing to consider allowing dance marathons. A deep antipathy to marathons was more typical. The summary written by Johnson's office based on his survey documents the objections and ordinances against marathons. Chiefs of police from all over the country were quoted anonymously in the report, which presented their responses under headings designed to suggest that the samples were representative of similar cities or geographical areas: "the middle west," "a large southern city," "a large industrial city in New England," and "an important city on the Pacific Coast." A typical commentary was received from a large southern city: "We have recently had a walkathon contest in our City and we were very pleased to get rid of it. We had numerous complaints from a cross section of the public and find that particularly our amusement concerns, theatres and so forth are very much opposed to these fly by night concerns inasmuch as they have a tendency to draw from their regular patronage." Other responses lamented the "undesirable element" attracted by the marathons and the negative effect this might have on the community. Still others commented that although marathons seemed relatively harmless and no complaints had been made to the Police Department, there was still a great deal of public sentiment against them.[3]

About a year after he conducted the survey, Johnson received a letter from Henry W. Toll of the American Legislator's Association, a nonpartisan organization established to promote legislative efficiency. Toll sent Johnson copies of enacted or pending antimarathon legislation from selected states. During their 1935 sessions, the state legislatures of Massachusetts, Indiana, Connecticut, Georgia, Iowa, Kansas, North

Dakota, South Dakota, Michigan, and Wisconsin all passed laws prohibiting dance marathons and other types of endurance amusements, including "skateathons" (later known as roller derbies), a new variation of dance marathons developed by the seasoned promoter Leo Seltzer. (See appendix.)[4]

Legislation pressed marathons from the beginning, but the pressure became more intense in the early 1930s. As a result of Hal J. Ross's shows, Texas in 1931 passed a law prohibiting any endurance contest of more than twenty-four hours duration. Also in 1931, Pennsylvania ceded control to individual boroughs to legislate marathons by adding an amendment to Act No. 145: "XXVI. Licensing Amusements—To regulate, license, fix the time of opening and closing, or prohibit theatrical exhibitions at which an admission or other fee is charged."[5] The typical state bill had multiple sponsors. For example, the Michigan bill, passed on May 31, 1935, was sponsored by the Welfare Guidance Bureau of Grand Rapids, ministerial groups, local chambers of commerce, and the Allied [motion picture] Theatres of Michigan.[6] Although it was claimed that the bills were passed in the name of public welfare, a number of organizations that sponsored them had obvious commerical interests at stake.

Like Texas, Maine, New Hampshire, and New York also passed laws limiting the number of hours persons could participate in endurance contests. The New Hampshire law applied only to minors and women; the Maine law had a provision stating that no marathon could be held except after a favorable vote of a city or town.[7] Indiana had a typical antimarathon ordinance:

Chapter No. 28
Approved February 6, 1935
An Act to prohibit "marathons," "marathon dance," "walkathons," "skateathons," and certain other mental and physical endurance contests and prescribing penalties of the violation thereof.

Section 1. Be it enacted by the General Assembly of the State of Indiana. That it shall be unlawful for any persons, firm, or corporation to maintain, operate, promote, conduct or advertise, or to aid in maintaining, operating, conducting, or advertising, or for any person to participate in any "marathon," "marathon dance," "walkathon," "skateathon," or any other mental or physical endurance contest or performance of a like or similar character or nature, under any name whatsoever.

Section 2. Nothing contained in this act shall be so construed as to apply to amateur or professional athletic events or contests or to high school, college or intercollegiate athletic contests or sports.

Section 3. Any person, firm or corporation who shall violate any of the provisions of this act shall be deemed guilty of a misdemeanor and upon conviction thereof shall be fined in any sum not less than fifty dollars and not more than two hundred dollars and each day on or during which such violation continues shall constitute a separate and distinct offence.[8]

The Indiana ordinance was exacting in its prohibition. All events that resembled dance marathons, no matter what the name, were outlawed. The ordinance also clearly differentiated between professional events developed for the purpose of making money and amateur events that had institutional or community affiliations. The determination to allow amateur community contests to continue underlined just how alien marathons had become to the communities in which they were staged. On the whole local communities feared and loathed outsiders who came in and, especially during hard times, extracted good money from local residents. Such visitors were felt to be flimflam artists, carpetbaggers, or crooks. These outsiders seduced and corrupted local youth, especially young women.

Dance marathons were thought to be homeless, wandering enterprises descending on "virgin" communities. Not only did they appear to many to attract "undesirables," they also seemingly posed a threat to the stable and permanent businesses upon which the community relied. Movie theaters, for example, were more or less permanent venues for one type of fairly consistent and carefully controlled entertainment. Movies could be screened before they were shown to the public, so that the authorities knew beforehand exactly what the film would show. Marathons, however, were more or less open-ended and unpredictable. Or at least they appeared so to local and state authorities. They were anything but permanent and were never able to develop any consistency, in spite of the best efforts of endurance-show attorney Richard S. Kaplan.

If a movie theater's economic stability was threatened by a marathon, it might very well have to shut down until the marathon had left town. By the same token, if a marathon promoter did not pay his bills, the businesses whose services he used were undermined. All in all, marathons were widely regarded as bad for local business. The community's fear of instability and change found an easy target in marathon promoters who had no ongoing investment in the welfare of local citizens. Concerns about the effects of marathons on the "morality" of the community were only in part about ethical behavior. Marathons were "wrong" to perform the pain and misery of the disadvantaged, but this situation was tolerated. However, combining such immorality with the possibility of an adverse effect on established businesses was unconscionable. Community leaders were wary of any situation that might worsen the already desperate economic conditions during the Depression.

Coupled with all this was the growing xenophobic fear of transients. This had long been part of the American consciousness, but it was heightened during the Depression. Although promoters and the professional contestants they brought with them were not indigent, neither were they part of the community. Thus they typically met with the same hostility as other transients. From the perspective of the Depression, promoters and contestants were easily seen as potential drains on already taxed resources. No one wanted to risk attracting the wandering unemployed. Who could guarantee that these people would move on after the show was finished? A potent demonstration of this rejection of the unemployed took place in 1932 when the Hoover administration called in the police to clear out the World War I veterans who had gathered in Washington to demand the passage of legislation giving them early payment for their war service. After the defeat of the legislation, thousands of veterans bivouacked on Anacostia Flats were run out of town with bayonets, tear gas, and tanks. Their shantytown was torched behind them.[9] They were not tramps or bums, just homeless and unemployed—a category that made the government suspect them of being communist agitators and that warranted their expulsion.

To be jobless and to protest was construed as anti-American behavior. Marathon promoters wanted above all to be American. They decorated their theaters with patriotic bunting, and the masters of ceremonies proclaimed the American-as-apple-pie virtues of the contests. But the bunting and the slick talk were now decoded by locals as little more than camouflage. Marathoners were seen as posing the same kind of threat to "real Americans" as the anti-Hoover veterans. Like the dispossessed characters in John Steinbeck's *Grapes of Wrath*, many marathon dancers had once been "respectable," if poor. Now they were treated as little more than bums, to be swept from one town to another by "good Americans." To a considerable number of "upstanding citizens," the marathoners resembled too closely for comfort the unemployed vagrants sweeping across the nation. As such, they had to be sent on their way.

The unemployed were now unpleasant reminders of the failure of the American dream. The terms on which marathons had been established were no longer current. The hope of an assured future upon which the prosperity of the 1920s was built had vanished with the Depression. Ebullience swiftly turned to terror, hope to anger, and welcome of the new to xenophobia. Against this, Kaplan's attempts to encourage the formation and success of the National Endurance Amusement Association (see chapter 6) were feeble at best. He seemed not to understand that no matter what legal rationale he might construct, the times were against him. But still he persisted. After it became clear that the NEAA had failed to transform dance marathons into a legitimate business, Kaplan began writing a *Billboard* column titled "Tidbits," in which he gave legal advice to dance marathoners and promoters. "Tidbits" began on October 19, 1935, with an editorial note explaining that the column was to serve promoters and contestants alike by presenting ideas for the betterment of the field, advising on the value of the latest developments, and offering "succulent thoughts regarding the industry and those in it."

Kaplan set the tone of the column with the following advice:

1. The name walkathon or walkashow must be dropped at once.
2. A name must be selected that is symbolic of the type of show to be conducted.
3. The entire form of the endurance contest must be altered.
4. Heat, in the form of whistle blowing, handkerchief snapping, and use of chains or straps, and other forms of heat now in use, must be forever eliminated.

The public is amusement hungry. They want amusement. And you can give it to them without the bosh and the bunk which has been heretofore employed.[10]

But basically Kaplan's suggestions were beside the point. Legislation outlawing all endurance dance contests, no matter what their name, was already on the books in many states and cities. And while it may have been true that the public was "amusement hungry," the kind of amusement they hungered for was rapidly changing. Marathons were big, noisy public shows. During the 1930s people began to opt increasingly for the dark, relatively quiet and private movies (whose apotheosis was achieved in the following decades by television). Movies gave people stars—bigger-than-life heroines and heroes—and narrative adventure with guaranteed outcome. The movies could also transport people imaginatively out of their daily lives to an endless variety of exotic times, places, and situations. Darkened movie palaces were the perfect place in which to dream away and forget the present. Marathons, by contrast, offered only more and more of the "here and now"—gritty, repetitious, and grueling, even if spiced up with vaudeville turns, sprays, and heat.

Kaplan's first vision of the NEAA had been as an organization that mirrored the most respectable civic groups, with a president, vice president, secretary, and so on. But clearly this had not worked, and he decided to fight local fire with local fire. In his "Tidbits" column, Kaplan continually argued for controlling marathons at the grass-roots level. He advised promoters to eliminate anything that could be perceived as offensive or dangerous and to drop the name "marathon" in favor of "derby." A derby would feature a series of athletic events, such as short hurdles, jumps, 100-yard dashes, and timed races with innovative variations. It would be staged against a background of "strict entertainments," such as songs, dances, instrumental music, stooging, and acrobatics.[11] It could be staged in the same sort of building as a marathon, he said, but the ring would have to be a little longer and wider. To comply with various regulatory ordinances and statutes, the "Mar-Vau," as he called it, would be limited to twenty-four hours, but it could still feature special matinees and evening shows. Teams would consist of "boys" and "girls" of legal age. They would compete in a series of athletic events, such as the 100-yard dash, hurdles, sprints over obstructions, and backward sprints. These contests would be interspersed with vaudeville acts. An emcee would preside. A staff of nurses, floor judges, and trainers would still be needed. Contestants would still take fifteen-minute rest periods between events. Even a roller-skating sprint could be added. Promoters must not forget about sanitation in the rest quarters, health care, and nourishing food for the contestants. Follow this plan, Kaplan argued, and all would go well. "That's the idea," he concluded. "Think it over and then go ahead and try to put it into effect. Here's the idea. I'm not selfish and I am not a promoter so all legitimate operators are welcome to this idea. It may be the salvation of the business."[12] No one seemed to take up his suggestions.

Kaplan believed his new format would allow for more "legitimate heat," as opposed to the "illegitimate heat" condemned in his fourth point. But he failed to understand that marathons as entertainment depended on the interaction between legitimacy and deception. What made marathons entertaining was an impure mixture of, and tension between, what was arranged, false, and "theatrical" and what was spontaneous, genuine, and "athletic."

At the end of his first column, Kaplan invited several key promoters to get behind his new ideas: Charlie Hayden, Fred Crockett, Walter Tebbetts, George Pughe, Hal J. Ross, Jack Steinel, Pop Dunlap, and Hugh Talbott.[13] Naming these men was apparently his way of identifying to *Billboard* readers those whom he saw as legitimate promoters. But even if identifying these men mattered to *Billboard*'s readers, the public and government authorities did not differentiate between "good" and "bad" promoters.

During the ten months the "Tidbits" column survived, Kaplan continually sought to eliminate the ambiguity between actual competition and staged heat. From his perspective, dramatization was the evil that had infected the wholesomeness of endurance shows. According to Kaplan, competition should not be theatrically amplified or augmented with straps or chains but should arise out of the struggle among the contestants. He never saw that the popularity of marathons rested on their gladiatorial displays, in which a class of people who were better off than the competitors watched those who were dramatizing their struggle to survive.

Kaplan continually urged promoters to challenge what he considered "unfair legislation" against endurance shows in the courts:

How many of you operators have been bumped up against this proposition?

An ordinance in a town limits the hours of public amusements to midnight and no shows on Sundays *but* makes an exception of *theatres*. This ordinance, of course hits at endurance contests. Should you run across that type of handicap, be assured that such an ordinance is discriminatory and unconstitutional, for the reason that

Stan West went from dance marathons to roller derbies which grew out of marathons. (Photo from the scrapbook of Richard Elliott)

it violates the constitutional guarantee of equal opportunity to all and attempts to discriminate between two types of amusements. Courts have frowned on this type of legislation and I feel certain that if a proper attack is made on such legislation thru injunctive proceedings you will be successful in opening your show.[14]

For the most part, Kaplan was using the word *theatre* to mean motion picture theaters. He knew that movie interests around the country were behind much of the legislation against dance marathons and endurance shows, and he was quick to point out the discriminatory and unconstitutional nature of much of the legislation.

Kaplan's pronouncements, however, did little to stem the tide of legislation. It is doubtful, in fact, that any of the opponents of marathons even read his column. And yet his writings in *Billboard* often seemed to be aimed directly at the enemies of marathons. Kaplan kept hammering away at the laws that made marathons illegal. As a lawyer he believed the battle to preserve and enhance marathons could be won in court.

The law does not tolerate the prohibition of something which may be regulated in such a manner as to overcome any evils which may be incidentally connected with it. Laws that pass the limit of a city's police power in that they discriminate and are unfair are, naturally, unreasonable and void. Municipalities are not general guardians of the public morals, and, therefore, may not unduly interfere with the liberty of the citizens by ordinance forbidding acts not unlawful or harmful per se. Where laws discriminate between equal rights of citizens, the laws will be held unconstitutional and void and an injunction will lie. (This is in the event that theatres are permitted to run in preference to endurance contests.)[15]

Kaplan could not see that the war over marathons was largely extralegal; the struggle to do away with them was being waged in the court of public opinion. Only after various special interests had convinced the public that marathons were evil, wrong, and dangerous could laws against the endurance shows be passed—and enforced. The "evils" associated with marathons by the public and the moralists may have been integral to the shows or incidental, mere "side effects." As public opinion turned against marathons, however, the evils were understood to be integral: it was not enough to govern the contests, the whole entertainment needed to be banned because it was bad for the public.

Kaplan failed to realize that municipalities during the Depression felt they had little control over events. One way they could demonstrate their authority was to ban "disorderly" events like marathons. At the same time, the public itself (not necessarily those who had attended marathons, but the "good citizens") had turned against the endurance shows. In such an atmosphere, promoters did not have a chance even if they went to court, as Kaplan suggested, and had the local laws thrown out as discriminatory and unconstitutional, which no doubt most of them were.

Promoters confirmed public disapproval by concentrating on burning up the remaining virgin territory with new variations on the shows designed to attract audiences. For a time reprises of early nonstop dancing experienced a fleeting revival. In Detroit, in August 1935, two women and three men danced 107 hours at the same ballroom where a Detroit record of 11 hours had been set twelve years earlier. But attendance was poor, and the last five dancers were solos who just would not give up. Finally the contest was called a draw, and the prize money was equally distributed.[16]

Kaplan urged changing the shows in a fundamental way, not just adding new variations to them. Unfortunately, his theatrical advice was not as cogent as his legal advice. Kaplan knew marathons had done good business in the past, but he did not understand the special nature of their theatricality. His suggestion of changing dance marathons into a series of athletic events against a background of special entertainments was something that many promoters had already tried in the early 1930s.[17]

From movie theaters Kaplan borrowed the idea of "bank night," during which cash prizes were awarded to the patrons whose ticket stubs were drawn. He also suggested amateur nights to attract local patronage.[18] After each suggestion, he repeatedly asked his readers what they thought. But *Billboard*'s letters column rarely had replies to Kaplan. "What do you think of the name Marvaudance or Vaudance as a new name for the endurance contest with all the present and past vicious features eliminated? Think it over and let me hear from you?"[19] Silence.

The fact was that marathons were stale. Unlike baseball, boxing, jazz, and other entertainments that had entered the American mainstream in the nineteenth and twentieth centuries, marathons had failed to enthrall people to such a degree that they acquired a permanent niche in popular culture. But surely hostile legislation and the charge of immorality are not the answer: there are many leisure activities (drinking, recreational drug use, gambling) that thrive despite legal and moral prohibition. Marathons never established a popular participatory base. People did not take part in amateur marathons in the same way that they played sandlot baseball. Nor were marathons ever seriously regarded as being a proud American innovation, like jazz. However simple it may seem, the truth is that dance marathons' day came and went.

Although Kaplan discussed antimarathon legislation, his advice was strangely severed from a sense of reality about marathons and those who promoted and danced in them. His relentless advice not only ignored the nature of good theatrical entertainment, it also lacked awareness of the effects of the Depression on public sentiment. He was constantly trying to resurrect the good old days—in fact, only a few years earlier—when marathons were thriving and the boys got together with wallets bulging their lapel pockets.

Despite the business going sour, some promoters were still living quite well. In November 1935, for example, Hal J. Ross was looking forward to his first vacation in seven years. He would spend it at his recently built home at 1945 North Normandie Avenue in Hollywood. Ross had produced approximately forty shows and had just closed one in Oklahoma City. He and singer Jane Shannon were still together, and she was now Jane Shannon Ross. Her dog, Midge, had just won a blue ribbon at the Oklahoma City Dog Show.[20]

Some performers were also doing fairly well. When he went out in fourth place in a 1935 California show, Stan West estimated that he made $250 from his final floor shower. "Yes, we had nice clothes, nice jewelry, and some of us had nice cars. You know what I mean. We could buy a car and travel, that kind of thing. The money was good because it went so far, two or three one-hundred-dollar bills would last you a long time."[21] But these success stories were flying against the wind. Overall, by the mid 1930s, dance marathons were a failing enterprise, although shows were staged sporadically well into the 1940s.

Kaplan recognized this and knew that unless big changes were made, marathons were finished. He grew more irritable and desperate as he realized that his advice for developing new types of shows was being ignored. He relied increasingly on platitudes and homilies to make his points. He urged contestants to stay loyal to the promoters for whom they worked: "After all, a mirror gives back the reflection of what stands before it." He admonished promoters to get along with each other: "A man can't throw mud at another without dirtying his own hands." And he reasoned: "When it is discovered that a red flag excites a bull, what do you do? Naturally you remove the red flag. Why not follow the same line of reasoning with reference to the endurance contest?"[22]

Kaplan's advice was uncannily like the moralizing of early reformers. But cleaning up the shows would come at the expense of all that made marathons lively and controversial. Kaplan advised getting rid of chains, straps, bandages, whistles, profanity, unkempt and ill-dressed contestants, and shouting and yelling into the radio microphone.[23] Cleaning up dance marathons to keep this form of entertainment alive seemed logical in that it answered the charges of the legislation banning them. But off-color jokes, questionable language, and desperate-appearing contestants made marathons what they were. The entertainment thrived on controversy. Spectators had flocked to marathons for precisely the same reasons moralists wanted them eliminated. For Kaplan it was a question of not only legitimacy but also respectability. Out of an estimated pool of twenty thousand contestants, he maintained that only eight hundred were "*real.*"[24] To these people he offered the following advice:

Contestants: Do you want to continue in this game? Do you want to help yourself and the operator? Then please observe the following important rules.

1. Don't use profanity in the quarters or on the floor.
2. Don't use any vulgarity.
3. Keep your hands to yourself.
4. Be clean at all times—physically and morally.
5. Help the nurse or trainer to keep the quarters clean at all times.
6. Don't smoke while on the floor or in your quarters. If you must smoke do so while on your hygiene periods. It looks better and safer for all.
7. Don't speak out of turn.
8. Don't agitate the floor.
9. Don't pay attention to wires from other operators asking you to leave the show you're with to join him.
10. Be courteous, friendly, gentlemanly and ladylike at all times. It pays.[25]

Kaplan also thought that talking across the rails to spectators warranted disqualification. Nor should contestants send or receive notes of any kind. Contact between the audience and contestants could arouse suspicion. If promoters had taken his advice they would have killed the shows outright. Marathons drew on interaction between spectators and participants, rule bending, sex, fierce competition, raw emotion, and hype. Kaplan apparently wanted them to be more like a Methodist Sunday service than the bawdy, raucous racket they had been.

According to Kaplan, floor judges and masters of ceremonies were also implicated in the decline. For them he had the following advice:

> Emcees: You can help by eliminating the familiarity you sometimes show on the stand. Eliminate the affectionate terms "honey" and "dearie" in speaking to a girl contestant from the stand. You're always in the spotlight. Your every act, your every word is carefully watched. Don't subject yourself or the show to criticism. There are too many critics always waiting to pounce upon any act or word and misconstrue the meaning intended.
>
> Floor judges: Familiarity between you and the contestants is absolutely *verboten!* Become familiar and you lose very bit of your power and control. You're a *judge.* As such you are presumed to be impartial. A bit of relaxation on your part and the floor is ruined—for you and the operator. Therefore, don't "kid" or joke with boys and girls on the floor. And when your hours of duty are over leave the building. Don't mingle with the contestants or the patrons. You'll find that everyone will respect you more for such an attitude. (Examples: Johnny Agrella, Maxie Capp, Larry Cappo.) [26]

Clearly, floor judges were making off-color jokes and insinuations about female contestants and betraying the fact that they were part of the show, not simply the referees.

Kaplan also railed against the double standards that demanded of marathons what was not asked of other forms of entertainment. Lacrosse, automobile racing, marathon running, boxing—all had been shown to be more injurious than marathon dancing. Ernie Schaaf had been killed in the boxing ring. Clay Weatherby lost control of his car and was killed at the Indianapolis race on May 30, 1935. Why should endurance dancing be discriminated against by the courts? [27] Kaplan cited the Indiana antimarathon law, passed in July 1935 to protect the health of participants, as an example of discriminatory legislation. [28] What went on at marathons was no worse than what went on at other sports.

The following is an actual excerpt from a daily paper and refers to the recent Joe Louis–Paulino Uzcudun fight: "One moment he was there for all to see, then, suddenly, he was gone, finished, inert, all but lifeless: his legs excommunicated, his head and shoulders bloody from the bosom to the hair line. The stockyards are more humane but not as artistic."

And the walkathon is barred because of alleged cruelty!!!
It's enough to exasperate a cockroach.[29]

Kaplan was exasperated. All of his advice had been to no avail. His column began to appear irregularly, and when he did write, his tone was increasingly sullen and glum. *Billboard* still carried an "Endurance Shows" section, but it now consisted mostly of briefs from different contestants put together by Don King. Stuff like: "Friends of the Kids in Bell, Calif. and Balboa Beach are inquiring as to the whereabouts of Patsy and Hobo, Elmer Dupree and Hughie Hendrixson."[30]

However wrongheaded Kaplan was, he was right about one thing: marathons were in danger of extinction, and one of the causes was dishonest promoters. Don King of *Billboard* wanted to expose some of these crooks. But there was a tacit agreement not to identify the chiselers by name. In the April 18, 1936, issue, King found a way around that restriction. Instead of naming names, King reprinted part of an article that had appeared in the *Milwaukee Journal* on April 4:

Seek arrest in walkathon. Racine police say showmen disappeared with prize money. Police here Saturday were trying to serve warrants on the promoters of the Race of Nations walkathon after four members of the orchestra, 12 contestants and several others connected with the show were left stranded without resources. Friday night was to have been pay day for the employees, as well as the date when contestants were to have received $1,750 in prizes as advertised in the walkathon posters. It was closing night of the show and all equipment was removed Saturday. Police are seeking I. L. Fox, S. M. Fox, and Louis Gluskey.[31]

Clearly marathon promoters were among their own worst enemies.

After the account of the Racine incident was published in *Billboard*, Kaplan wrote again saying that his April 25, 1936, "Tidbits" column might be his last: "If this is the last issue of Tidbits blame those who have hurt the game."[32] But it was not the last. In his next column on

May 9, Kaplan said that he had received many letters requesting that he continue writing as long as possible. But only the future of the shows, he cautioned, would determine how long the column could last. This was quite accurate because the "Endurance Shows" and "Tidbits" columns were supported by advertising for dance marathons, and this source of revenue was rapidly diminishing. Between May 9 and August 22, there were five "Tidbits" columns. By this time, Kaplan was repeating himself, recycling old news. On August 22, he pleaded for readers to patronize the advertising columns of *Billboard* in order for "Tidbits" to continue, but his plea came too late.[33] Kaplan had written his last column.

An occasional small news column continued in the back of the trade journal. One of the last *Billboard* notices concerning marathons appeared in 1939, in the "Final Curtain" section. It was an announcement of the murder of Charles Hayden outside the marathon he was staging in Chicago's Park Casino. There was no speculation about who shot him or for what reason. Those in the know understood that Hayden was working a territory that did not belong to him.

Dishonest promoters were probably mostly responsible for the banning of dance marathons. Movie theater interests surely saw marathons as competition. But this alone was not enough to galvanize legislators into passing laws against marathons. The world had changed radically between 1923 and the 1930s. The loose living, gangsterism, and devil-may-care attitudes of the high-flying 1920s steadily changed into the grim, grind-it-out 1930s. Instead of a tolerance supported by prosperity, social reform and fascist politics together with xenophobia and red baiting steadily rose during the 1930s. American fascism, preached by Father Coughlin and others, joined with the Ku Klux Klan, America Firsters, and a whole cadre of reactionaries to clamp down on behaviors that only a few years before had been celebrated and enjoyed. The public and legislators no longer saw the "fun" of marathons. Instead they came to fear the physical danger to contestants and spectators, to hate the rigged shows, to deplore the poor health conditions, and to want to do away with fly-by-night promoters. Movie theater owners seized the opportunity and strongly lobbied lawmakers to ban the endurance shows. The legislators were only too happy to oblige, and few members of the public cared enough to protest.

As important as these overt causes for the demise of dance marathons is the fleeting and ephemeral nature of such popular entertainments

Like roller derbies, speed derbies grew out of dance marathons. Both contests
emphasized dramatized athletic endurance with little special entertainment.
(Photo from the scrapbook of Richard Elliott)

that characterize a particular period.[34] During the Depression dance
marathons had been a performance of the poverty, cruelty, and chance
survival of the disenfranchised. They were both an example and a
mockery of the American dream of success. The passion for winning
was joined with—was even transformed into—the struggle for survival.
Spectators and contestants had lived and breathed the economic, social,
and theatrical forces that created marathons. They were willing to reveal their feelings about their own plight by passionately watching a theatricalized version of what America was offering them. The central contradiction of dance marathons—between the actual struggles and the
staged dramatizations—was not resolvable by either the spectators or
the contestants. The contradiction was the essence of dance marathons'
unique theatricality and doomed the efforts of the National Endurance
Amusement Association to make the shows into a legitimate business.

The shows that did continue into the 1940s changed enormously. They were called speed derbies or steeplechase derbies and were adapted from the elimination features that had come in with walkathons. Speed derbies featured contestants in running shorts and helmets, performing athletic stunts in a circular fashion on a floor set up with pylons. These shows were cousins of the dance marathon, but they were very different in appearance and tone. They were more like the roller derbies of the 1940s and 1950s than the "classic" dance marathons of the early 1930s. They lacked the social events (mock weddings), slices of private life (sleeping and eating), and flirtation with the audience, as well as a variety of popular entertainments, all unified by the spectacle of an ongoing, seemingly endless competition. The new derbies were direct, simple, and brutal rather than multiplex, ironic, and sly. The classic marathons had been, in fact, a vibrant distorting mirror, refracting a society's desires, entertainments, working habits, scams, and brassy personalities.

Appendix
Legislation Relevant to Dance Marathons

The following summary of state legislation relating to dance marathons and the text of seven laws were sent in 1935 by Henry Toll, a member of the American Legislators' Association, to Bascom Johnson of the "Legal and Protective Measures Activities" of the American Social Hygiene Association. The examples of municipal ordinances that follow were sent by chiefs of police in various U.S. cities to Bascom Johnson in response to a survey concerning municipal marathon laws.

STATE LEGISLATION

During their 1935 sessions, many state legislatures have shown an interest in prohibiting "marathon" dances and similar endurance contests, although a few states passed such legislation as early as 1931.

One of the first states to take cognizance of this problem was Texas, which passed a law in 1931 prohibiting any endurance contest of more than 24 hours duration, but exempting from the provisions of the act athletic contests of the schools and colleges, as well as trial tests of materials and machinery. This law was changed in 1935 to limit any one such contest to 7 days duration, to limit participation of any contestant therein to 24 hours, and to add certain other provisions.

In 1933, Maine, New Hampshire, and New York passed laws limiting the number of consecutive hours during which any person may participate in an endurance contest. The New Hampshire law, however, applies only to women and to minors. The law in Maine also has had a provision stating that "no such marathon dance . . . shall be held in any city or town excepting after a vote therefor by the legal voters of said city or town."

Thus far in 1935, six states—Georgia, Indiana, Iowa, Kansas, North Dakota, and South Dakota—have enacted legislation prohibiting marathon dances. According to present information similar measures are now pending in Florida, Michigan, Minnesota, North Carolina, Ohio, Rhode Island, and Wisconsin.

One of the most interesting developments in connection with this subject is the proposal made by Senator James G. Moran of Massachusetts that the General Court designate a special joint committee to make an investigation of so-called marathon dancing contests and of the regulation of tourist camps. A copy of Senator Moran's order is reprinted.

There are also reproduced herewith the laws as passed in Indiana, New York, Pennsylvania and Texas, as well as the bills which have been introduced in Connecticut and Wisconsin. The acts which have been passed or are pending in most of the states mentioned above, but which are not reprinted, are essentially similar to either the Indiana or Connecticut laws.

Massachusetts

Journal of the Senate
Monday, January 21, 1935
Mr. Moran offered the following order, and under the joint rule, it was referred to the committees on Rules of the two branches, acting concurrently, to wit:

Ordered, That a special joint committee, to consist of three members of the Senate to be designated by the President thereof, and five members of the House of Representatives to be designated by the Speaker thereof, be appointed to make an investigation into the conduct of so-called marathon dancing contests, Walkathon contests, and similar contests, and also the regulation of overnight camps, for the purpose of determining whether these contests and camps are being conducted in a manner which is harmful to the health and morals of our people. The committee shall report to the General Court by filing its findings, together with its recommendations and drafts of legislation necessary to carry such recommendations into effect, with the Clerk of the Senate on or before March first in the current year.

(This is still before the Rules Committee.)

Indiana

Chapter No. 28

Approved February 6, 1935

An Act to prohibit "marathons," "marathon dances," "walkathons," "skatathons," and certain other mental and physical endurance contests and prescribing penalties for the violation thereof.

Section 1. Be it enacted by the General Assembly of the State of Indiana, That it shall be unlawful for any person, firm, or corporation to maintain, operate, promote, conduct or advertise, or to aid in maintaining, operating, promoting, conducting or advertising, or for any person to participate in any "marathon," "marathon dance," "walkathon," "skatathon," or any other mental or physical endurance contest or performance of a like or similar character or nature, under any name whatsoever.

Section 2. Nothing contained in this act shall be so construed as to apply to amateur or professional athletic events or contests or to high school, college or intercollegiate athletic contests or sports.

Section 3. Any person, firm or corporation who shall violate any of the provisions of this act shall be deemed guilty of a misdemeanor and upon conviction thereof shall be fined in any sum not less than fifty dollars and not more than two hundred dollars and each day on or during which such violation continues shall constitute a separate and distinct offense.

New York

New York Act Prohibiting Marathons

Chapter 418, Laws of 1933

(Approved by Governor Lehman, April 24, 1933)

An Act to amend the penal law, in relation to prohibiting marathon dance contests and participation therein.

The people of the State of New York, represented in Senate and Assembly, do enact as follows:

Section 1. The penal law is hereby amended by inserting therein a new section, to be section 833 to read as follows:

Section 833. *Marathon dance contest and participation therein prohibited.* Any person, firm, association, or corporation promoting, conducting, or advertising and each person participating in a marathon dance contest or performance continuing or intended to continue for a period of more than eight consecutive hours, whether or not an admission fee is charged and/or a prize is or is not to be awarded to one or more participants for participation therein, is guilty of a misdemeanor.

This Act shall take effect September 1, 1933.

Pennsylvania

Act No. 145
Session laws of 1931.
An Act
To amend sections . . . one thousand two hundred two . . . entitled "An act concerning boroughs . . . ". . . by authorizing the fixing of the time of opening and closing certain exhibitions . . .

Section 13. That clauses twenty-six . . . of section one thousand two hundred two of said act are hereby amended to read as follows:

XXVI. Licensing Amusements—To regulate, license, fix the time of opening and closing, or prohibit theatrical exhibitions, amusements, dances, at which an admission or other fee is charged and other exhibitions. . . .

Texas

As Passed—Chapter 26—Page 131, Laws, 2d Called Session, 43d Legislature, 1934

An Act to regulate the conducting in public competition for prizes, awards, or admission fees, any personal, physical or mental endurance contests; regulating the manner in which contestants may participate in such contests; exceptions to this act; declaring that any house, structure, building, place or open air space that is being used for purposes in violation of the provisions of this act is declared to be a nuisance; providing that any person who knowingly maintains or assists in maintaining of such a place is guilty of maintaining a nuisance, authorizing the Attorney General or the district attorney or county attorney under certain circumstances to enjoin and abate such nuisance; prescribing the character of judgment that shall be entered against the continuance of such nuisance; providing certain conditions with reference to bonds to be furnished in such cases; repealing Chapter 204, page 337 of the Acts of the Forty-second Legislature, 1931; prescribing penalties for violations; providing that if any portion of this act shall be declared unconstitutional it shall not affect the validity of the remainder; and declaring an emergency.

Be it enacted by the Legislature of the State of Texas:

Section 1. It shall hereafter be unlawful for any person to conduct in public competition for prizes, awards or admission fees, any personal, physical or mental endurance contest that continues longer than twenty-four (24) hours.

Section 2. It shall hereafter be unlawful for any person to conduct, within any period of one hundred sixty-eight (168) hours, in public competition for prizes, awards, or admission fees, more than one (1) such personal, physical or mental endurance contest at the same place or location, and in which any of the same contestants engage.

Section 3. It shall hereafter be unlawful for any contestant to engage in any personal, physical or mental endurance contest for a period of longer than twenty-four (24) hours.

Section 4. It shall hereafter be unlawful for any person to engage, within any period of one hundred sixty-eight (168) hours, in more than one (1) personal, physical or mental endurance contest which is conducted in the same place or location.

Section 5. Each promoter of or person conducting any personal, physical or mental endurance contest in public competition for prizes, awards or admission fees, who shall violate any provision of this Act, or any person who shall enter any contest that violates any provision of this act, or any person who shall violate any provision of this act, shall be fined not less than $100.00 nor more than $1,000.00 for each offense, or confined in the county jail not less than thirty (30) days nor more than ninety (90) days, or by both such fine and imprisonment.

Section 6. The provisions of this act shall not apply to any athletic contest of schools, colleges or universities of the State, nor to any trial contest for the purpose of testing the strength and capacity of materials and machinery of any kind.

Section 7. Any house, structure, building, place or open air space that is being used for the purposes in violation of the provisions of this act is hereby declared to be a common nuisance. Any person who knowingly maintains or assists in the maintaining of such a place is guilty of maintaining a nuisance.

Section 8. Whenever the Attorney General, or the district or county attorney had reliable information that such a nuisance exists, the Attorney General or the district or county attorney under his direction, shall file in the name of the State in the county where the nuisance is alleged to exist against whoever maintains such nuisance to abate and enjoin the same. If judgment be in favor of the State, then judgment shall be rendered enjoining the defendants from maintaining the same, and ordering the said house to be closed for one year from the date of said judgment, unless the defendants in said suit, or the owner, tenant, or lessee of said property make bond payable to the State at the county seat of the county where such nuisance is alleged to exist, in the penal sum of not less than one thousand nor more than five thousand dollars, with sufficient sureties to be approved by the judge trying the case, conditioned that the facts prohibited in this law shall not be done or permitted to be done in said house. On violation of any condition of such bond, the whole sum may be recovered as a penalty in the name and for the State in the county where such conditions are violated, all such suits to be brought by the district or county attorney of such county.

Section 9. Chapter 204, page 337, of the Acts of the Forty-second Legislature, 1931, otherwise known as Article 614-A of the Revised Criminal Statutes of the State of Texas, is hereby in all things repealed.

Section 10. If any section, sub-section, sentence, clause, word, or phrase of this Act is for any reason held to be unconstitutional, such holding shall not affect the validity of the remaining portions of this Act, which are hereby declared distinct and severable.

Connecticut

H.B538 Judiciary, General Assembly, January Session, A.D., 1935

An Act Concerning An Act to Prohibit Marathon Dances, Walkathons, and Skatathons

Be it enacted by the Senate and House of Representatives in General Assembly convened:

Section 1. It shall be unlawful for any person or persons, firm or corporation, to advertise, operate, maintain, attend, participate in, promote and aid in the advertising, operating, maintaining or promoting any mental or physical endurance contest, exhibition, performance or show, in the nature of a "Marathon," "Walkathon," "Skatathon," or any other such endurance contest, exhibition, performance, or show of a like or similar nature, whether or not an admission is charged and/or a prize is or is not to be awarded to one or more participants for participation therein, continuing or intended to continue for a period of more than four (4) consecutive hours in any twenty-four (24) hours.

Section 2. Any person or persons, firm or corporation, participating in, attending, promoting, advertising, operating, maintaining, or aiding any such contest, exhibition, performance or show, and violating any of the provisions of this Act, shall be guilty of a gross misdemeanor and punished by imprisonment in the County Jail for not less than six (6) months or more than twelve (12) months and by fine of not more than One Thousand dollars ($1,000.00) or by both.

Wisconsin

In Assembly, No. 218, A
February 15, 1935—introduced by Mr. Mulder
Referred to Committee on Public Welfare
A Bill
To create section 352.48 of the statutes, relating to endurance contests and providing a penalty.

The people of the state of Wisconsin, represented in senate and assembly, do enact as follows:

Section 1. A new section is added to the statutes to read: 52.48 Certain Endurance Contests Prohibited; Penalty. Any dancing, walking, or roller-skating contest wherein the endurance of any participant or participants is matched against any other participant or against a period of time or where the period of time of endurance of any person is to be ascertained in any manner whatever is hereby declared unlawful whether or not any prize or admission fee is offered or given. Any person who shall advertise, promote, conduct, participate in, or attend any dancing, walking or roller-skating contest wherein the endurance of any participant is matched against any other participant or against a period of time or where the period of time of endurance is to be ascertained in any manner whatever, whether or not any prize or admission fee is offered, given or required, shall be deemed guilty of a misdemeanor and upon conviction thereof shall be punished by a fine of not less than one hundred dollars or more than five hundred dollars or by imprisonment in the county jail for not to exceed one year, or by both such fine and imprisonment.

Section 2. This act shall take effect upon passage and publication.

MUNICIPAL ORDINANCES

Oakland, California

(Received in letter from Mr. Bodie A. Wallman, chief of police, City of Oakland, California, March 19, 1954)
Article 6.
Gatherings and Meetings
Sec. 3-6.03 Marathons. It shall be unlawful for any person within the City of Oakland, to promote, conduct, carry on or take part in, any public exhibition of endurance contests commonly known and designated as "walktahons" or "dance marathons" or "skate marathons."

Atlantic City, New Jersey

(Received in letter from Mr. James McManamin, acting chief of police, Atlantic City, N.J., April 3, 1934)
Ordinance
No. 11
City of Atlantic City, New Jersey
Introduced by Mayor Bacharach
June 23, 1932
"An Ordinance to hereafter prohibit Exhibition Dances, Endurance Dances, and Dance Contests, commonly known and designated as 'Marathon Dance' and/or 'Marathon Contest'; regulating such dances already licensed by the City and providing penalties for the violation thereof."
The Board of Commissioners of the City of Atlantic City do ordain:
Section 1. That on and after passing of this ordinance it shall be unlawful for any person, persons, firm, co-partnership, association or corporation to conduct, manage or operate within the limits of the City of Atlantic City any Exhibition Dances, Endurance Dances, and Dance Contests, commonly known and designated as "Marathon Dance" and/or "Marathon Contest."
Section 2. That any person, persons, firm, association, co-partnership, or corporation violating any provisions of this Ordinance, shall, upon conviction thereof, pay a fine not exceeding $100.00 for the first offense, and a fine not exceeding $100.00 for the violation of each and every offense thereafter, and, upon default in the payment of any first or subsequent fine herein provided, shall be imprisoned in the City or County Jail for a period not exceeding 30 days.

Section 3. That in addition to the penalties herein provided, the Board of Commissioners of Atlantic City shall have the right to revoke any license heretofore granted by the City to conduct, manage or operate Exhibition Dances, Endurance Dances, and Dance Contests, commonly known and designated as "Marathon Dance" and/or "Marathon Contest"; when in their judgment it is in the interest of public welfare, public health, safety and morals, desirable to revoke same; provided, however, that before any license is revoked, the Board of Commissioners shall give at least five days written notice to the licensee of the fact that it shall conduct a hearing at a given time and place for the reasons set forth in said notice why the license should not be revoked. The licensee shall have the right to appear in person, with his witnesses and counsel, and present such proof as he may desire.

Section 4. This Ordinance is hereby declared to be necessary in the interests of public welfare, morals, health and safety.

Section 5. That the provisions of this Ordinance, with the exceptions as to penalties, Section 2, and the right of revocation, Section 3, shall not relate to or apply to licenses heretofore granted by the City to anyone to conduct such Exhibition Dances, Endurance Dances, and Dance Contests, commonly known and designated as "Marathon Dance" and/or "Marathon Contest," at the time of the passage of this Ordinance.

Section 6. All ordinances or parts of ordinances inconsistent herewith be and the same are hereby repealed to extent of such inconsistencies.

Section 7. This Ordinance shall take effect immediately after its final passage and publication.

Passed at a regular meeting of City Commission July 7, 1932.

Harry Bacharach, Mayor

William S. Cuthbert, Louis Kuehnle, J. A. Paxson, Robert L. Warke, Jr., Commissioners of Atlantic City.

Attest:

Bertram E. Whitman, City Clerk.

Published July 8, 1932—Press.

Published prior to passage June 25, 1932—Press.

Los Angeles, California

(Received from Mr. James E. Davis, chief of police, City of Los Angeles, California March 6, 1934)

Ordinance No. 61,653

As amended by Ordinance No. 71.181

An Ordinance prohibiting Marathon dancing contests, exhibitions or races and other contests or exhibitions of endurance in dancing.

The People of the City of Los Angeles do ordain as follows:

Section 1. (As amended by Ordinance No. 71,181 approved April 1, 1932.) An Ordinance prohibiting Marathon dancing contests, exhibitions or races, and other contests or exhibitions of endurance in dancing.

It shall be unlawful for any person, firm or corporation to conduct or carry on any so-called Marathon dancing contest, exhibition or race or any contest or exhibition of endurance in dancing, or any Walkathon or any contest of a similar nature, continuing for more than 24 hours, within the city limits of the City of Los Angeles.

Sec. 2. (As amended by Ordinance No. 71.181, approved April 1, 1932.) It shall be unlawful for any person or association to participate in any so-called Marathon dancing contest, exhibition or race or in any contest or exhibition of endurance in dancing or any Walkathon or any contest of a similar nature, within the City limits of the City of Los Angeles.

Sec. 3. That any person, firm or corporation violating any of the provisions of this ordinance shall be deemed guilty of a misdemeanor and upon conviction thereof shall be punishable by a fine of not more than Five Hundred Dollars or by imprisonment in the city jail for a period of not more than six months, or by both such fine and imprisonment.

Sec. 4. The City Clerk shall certify to the passage of this ordinance by a unanimous vote and cause the same to be published once in the Los Angeles *Daily Journal.*

I hereby certify that the foregoing ordinance was passed by the Council of the City of Los Angeles by the unanimous vote of all the members of said Council present, there being no less than twelve members present, at its meeting of July 25, 1928.

Robt. Dominguez, City Clerk

Approved this 26th day of July, 1928.

Wm. G. Bonelli, Acting Mayor

Minneapolis, Minnesota

(Received in letter from Mr. M. J. Johannes, superintendent of police, Police Department, Minneapolis, Minn., March 7, 1934)

An Ordinance

To amend an ordinance entitled "An ordinance regulating licenses in the City of Minneapolis," passed April 29, 1887, as subsequently amended.

The City Council of the City of Minneapolis do ordain as follows:

Section 1. That the first paragraph of Section 5 of an ordinance entitled, "An ordinance regulating licenses in the City of Minneapolis," passed April 29, 1887, as subsequently amended, and as the same appears on page 655 of the 1872–1925 compilation of Minneapolis City Charter and Ordinances, be and the same is hereby amended so as to read as follows:

"Section 5. That no caravan, menagerie, circus or other show, exhibition or performance, or business for which the price of a license is hereinafter stated, shall be held, exhibited, or carried on within said City, unless a license therefor shall be previously obtained, as hereinafter provided. Provided, that no license or permit shall be granted to conduct any so-called dance marathon or walkathon, or any combination of either of them. The rules of such licenses are fixed as follows."

Section 2. This ordinance shall take effect and be in force from and after its publication.

Passed August 26, 1932. Sidney Benson, Vice President of the Council and President pro tem.

Approval August 29, 1932. William A. Anderson, Mayor.

Attest: Cham. C. Swanson, City Clerk.

Somerville, Massachusetts

City of Somerville

Ordinance No. 102

An Ordinance relative to dancing exhibitions, public amusements, and entertainments.

Be it ordained by the Board of Aldermen of the City of Somerville, as follows—

Section 1. No person, firm or corporation shall conduct in any hall or other public place in the City of Somerville any dancing exhibition or other form of public amusement such as a walkathon or marathon exhibition wherein the participants therein are permitted to engage in an endurance contest, or wherein persons engaged in such a contest continue to dance or walk or engage in said contest for more than four hours in any one day; nor shall any amusement or entertainment conducted in connection with or as part of such dancing or walking contest be permitted after twelve o'clock midnight on any week day except Saturday, on which day said walking or dancing contest or amusement or entertainment conducted in connection therewith on the premises or place of amusement shall cease at 11:45 p.m.

Section 2. No person shall engage in or participate in any such dancing or walking contest, or in any amusement or entertainment conducted or carried on, on the premises used for said dancing or walking contest, after twelve o'clock on any week day except Saturday 11:45 p.m.: provided, however, that no person engaging in such dancing or walking contest shall be permitted to continue therein for more than four hours in any one day.

Section 3. Any person violating any of the provisions of this ordinance shall be liable to a penalty not exceeding twenty dollars for each offense.

Section 4. This ordinance shall take effect upon its passage.

A true copy of an ordinance approved conditionally, May 22, 1933.

Attest: Norman E. Corwin, city Clerk, May 26

Birmingham, Alabama

Ordinance No. 82-F.

An Ordinance to Amend Section 5511 1/2 of the General Code of the City of Birmingham of 1930.

Be it ordained by the Commission of the City of Birmingham that Section 5511 1/2 of the General Code of the City of Birmingham of 1930 be, and the same hereby is, amended so as to read as follows:

Section 5511 1/2. Endurance Contests.—It shall be unlawful for any person to engage in any test of endurance in tree or pole sitting, or in any exhibition of wire walking or building climbing in view of any public highway, and it shall also be unlawful for any person, firm or corporation to conduct, engage in or participate in, any test or contest in walking or dancing, by whatsoever name called, which shall endure either continuously or intermittently for a period of more than twenty-four hours.

Milwaukee, Wisconsin

(Received in letter from Mr. J. G. Laubenheimer, chief of police, Milwaukee, Wisc., March 9, 1934)

The following ordinance was passed by the Common Council of this city:

"Section 1075.5. The holding, showing or exhibiting of dance marathons or walkathons is hereby prohibited within the corporate limits of the City of Milwaukee.

"Section 1075.6. Any person, persons, firm, association or corporation holding, showing or exhibiting a dance marathon or walkathon shall upon conviction thereof be punished by a fine not exceeding two hundred dollars, or in default of payment thereof by a sentence not exceeding ninety days in the county jail."

Notes

1. COMMON HEROES

1. Robert S. McElvaine, *The Great Depression* (New York: Times Books, 1984), p. 10.
2. Ibid., p. 11.
3. *New York Times*, 2 April 1923, p. 1. Cummings exemplifies the "instant" hero described by Mertz in the epigraph to this chapter. See Charles Mertz, *The Great American Bandwagon: A Study of Exaggerations* (New York: Literary Guild, 1928), pp. 215–16.
4. Ibid.
5. Ibid.
6. Frank M. Calabria, "The Dance Marathon Craze," *Journal of Popular Culture* 10 (Summer 1976): 55.
7. Anonymous, "Tripping the Long, Hard Fantastic for a Record," *Literary Digest* 77/5 (5 May 1923): 44.
8. Paul Sann, *Fads, Follies and Delusions* (New York: Bonanza Books, 1967), p. 76.
9. Ibid., p. 39.
10. Ibid., p. 40.
11. Ibid.
12. Ibid., p. 44.
13. Ibid.
14. Lewis A. Erenberg, *Steppin' Out: New York Nightlife and the Transformation of American Culture* (Chicago: University of Chicago Press, 1981), p.236.
15. *New York Times*, 5 April 1923, p. 14.
16. *New York Times*, 13 April 1923, p. 6.
17. *New York Times*, 29 April 1923, sec. 4, p. 1.

18. *New York Times,* 11 April 1923, p. 23.
19. *New York Times,* 15 April 1923, p. 1. "Blue laws" were first established in colonial New England.
20. Ibid.
21. *New York Times,* 16 April 1923, p. 4.
22. *New York Times,* 15 April 1923, p. 2.
23. Ibid.
24. "Tripping the Long, Hard Fantastic for a Record," p. 43.
25. William E. Leuchtenburg, *The Perils of Prosperity* (Chicago: University of Chicago Press, 1958), p. 160.
26. Erenberg, *Steppin' Out,* p. 151.
27. Ibid., p. 147.
28. Mertz, *Great American Bandwagon,* p. 215.
29. Kathy Peiss, *Cheap Amusements* (Philadelphia: Temple University Press, 1986), p. 93.
30. Ibid., p. 72.
31. Ibid., p. 73.
32. *New York Times,* 24 April 1923, p. 23.
33. *New York Times,* 16 April 1923, p. 1.
34. Ibid.
35. Ibid.
36. Ibid.
37. *New York Times,* 18 April 1923, p. 6.
38. "Tripping the Long, Hard Fantastic for a Record," p. 43.
39. *New York Times,* 19 April 1923, p. 22.
40. Ibid.
41. *New York Times,* 18 April 1923, p. 6.
42. *New York Times,* 19 April 1923, p. 22.
43. "Tripping the Long, Hard Fantastic for a Record," p. 43.
44. *New York Times,* 19 April 1923, p. 22.
45. Ibid.
46. *New York Times,* 26 June 1923, p. 19.
47. Ibid.
48. *New York Times,* 16 April 1923, p. 1.
49. *New York Times,* 29 April 1923, sec. 4, p. 1.
50. Ibid.
51. *New York Times,* 17 April 1923, p. 8.
52. "Tripping the Long, Hard, Fantastic for a Record," p. 44.
53. *New York Times,* 19 April 1923, p. 22.
54. Ibid.
55. Ibid., p. 1.

56. "Tripping the Long Hard Fantastic for a Record," p. 44.
57. *New York Times,* 23 April 1923, p. 17.
58. Ibid.
59. *New York Times,* 10 May 1923, p. 17.
60. *New York Times,* 28 May 1923, p. 3.
61. *New York Times,* 11 June 1923, p. 2.

2. THE DANCE DERBY OF THE CENTURY

1. Tania Modleski, *Loving with a Vengeance* (New York: Methuen, 1984).
2. Paul Sann, *Fads, Follies and Delusions* (New York: Bonanza Books, 1967), p. 57.
3. Joseph Kaye, "Dance of Fools," *Dance Magazine* (February 1931): 13.
4. Frank M. Calabria, "The Dance Marathon Craze," *Journal of Popular Culture* 10 (Summer 1976): 59.
5. Sann, *Fads, Follies and Delusions,* p. 57.
6. Jimmy Scott, "We Danced All Night—And All Day!" *Ballroom Dance Magazine* (July 1961): 8.
7. *New York Evening Graphic,* 27 June 1928.
8. *New York Times,* 11 June 1928, p. 23.
9. Scott, "We Danced All Night," p. 8.
10. *New York Times,* 10 June 1928, p. 17.
11. William E. Leuchtenburg, *The Perils of Prosperity, 1914–32* (Chicago: University of Chicago Press, 1958), p. 226.
12. *New York Times,* 11 June 1928, p. 11.
13. Scott, "We Danced All Night," p. 9.
14. *New York Times,* 10 June 1928, p. 17.
15. Scott, "We Danced All Night," p. 9.
16. *New York Times,* 10 June 1928, p. 17.
17. Ibid.
18. *New York Times,* 12 June 1928, p. 12.
19. Ibid.
20. *New York Times,* 13 June 1928, p. 26.
21. Scott, "We Danced All Night," p. 23.
22. Ibid., p. 21.
23. Ibid., p. 9.
24. Ibid., p. 20.
25. Ibid., p. 21.
26. Glenn Shirley, *"Hello, Suckers!": The Story of Texas Guinan* (Austin, Texas: Eakin Press, 1989), p. 49.
27. Scott, "We Danced All Night," p. 9.

28. Shirley, *"Hello, Suckers!"* p. 46.

29. Ibid., p. 58.

30. Ibid. p. 47.

31. *New York Times,* 16 June 1928, p. 19.

32. Ibid.

33. *New York Times,* 18 June 1928, p. 11.

34. *New York Times,* 19 June 1928, p. 29.

35. *New York Times,* 20 June 1928, p. 27.

36. Ibid.

37. Ibid.

38. Ibid., p. 19.

39. *New York Times,* 13 June 1928, p. 12.

40. *New York Times,* 21 June 1928, p. 29.

41. *Nation,* 23 June 1928, p. 9.

42. *New York Times,* 21 June 1928, p. 29.

43. *New York Times,* 22 June 1928, p. 25.

44. Thomas Kessner, *Fiorello H. La Guardia and the Making of Modern New York* (New York: Penguin Books, 1989), p. 155.

45. Ibid., p. 233.

46. Ibid., p. 159.

47. Ibid., p. 157.

48. Robert McElvaine, *The Great Depression* (New York: Times Books, 1984), p. 22.

49. Ibid.

50. Ibid., p. 18.

51. Kessner, *Fiorello H. La Guardia,* p. 156.

52. *New York Times,* 30 June 1928, p. 19.

3. FOR NO GOOD REASON

1. Arnold Gingrich, "Poor Man's Night Club," *Esquire* (Autumn 1933): 61.

2. Ibid.

3. George Eells, interview with author, New York City, 18 September 1986.

4. Ibid.

5. Stan West, interview with author, Burbank, California, 22 May 1986.

6. Stan West, "A Hot Time in Hampden," *Down East* (December 1988): 120.

7. Ibid., p. 87.

8. Ibid.

9. Ibid.

10. West, interview with author, 22 May 1986.

11. Carol Martin, "Betty Herndon Meyer," *New Observations* 39 (1986): 7.

12. Carol Martin, "Richard Elliott," *New Observations* 39 (1986): 7.

13. June Havoc, *Early Havoc* (New York: Simon and Schuster, 1959), p. 80.

14. Norma Jasper, interview with author, Van Nuys, California, 16 May 1986.

15. Betty Freund, letter to author, 2 November 1985.

16. Warren Susman, *Culture as History* (New York: Pantheon Books, 1984).

17. Martin, "Richard Elliott," p. 8.

18. Gingrich, "Poor Man's Night Club," p. 61.

19. Everett Perlman and G. W. Nelson, *The Marathon Guide* (Minneapolis: Privately printed, 1928), p. 20.

20. Ibid., p. 16.

21. Ibid., p. 17.

22. Ibid., p. 18.

23. Ibid., p. 17.

24. George Eells, "Some 20,000 Were in 'Marathon Dance' Biz at Zenith of Craze," *Variety*, 7 January 1970, p. 154.

25. Perlman and Nelson, *Marathon Guide*, p. 29.

26. Eells, interview with author, 18 September 1986.

27. Ibid.

28. Jean Stearns and Marshall Stearns, *Jazz Dance* (New York: Schirmer Books, 1968), p. 316.

29. Havoc, *Early Havoc*, p. 42.

30. Eells, interview with author, *New Observations* 39 (1986): 17.

31. Eells, "Some 20,000 Were in 'Marathon Dance' Biz," p. 154.

32. Eells, *New Observations* interview, p. 17.

4. PRIVATE FANTASY AND PUBLIC AMBIVALENCE

1. Lewis A. Erenberg, *Steppin' Out: New York Nightlife and the Transformation of American Culture* (Chicago: University of Chicago Press, 1981), p. 236.

2. Lois Banner, *Women in Modern America: A Brief History* (New York: Harcourt Brace Jovanovich, 1984), pp. 161–62.

3. Erenberg, *Steppin' Out*, p. 236.

4. Ibid.

5. Anonymous, "Tripping the Long, Hard Fantastic for a Record," *Literary Digest* 77/5 (5 May 1923): 44.

6. Erenberg, *Steppin' Out*, p. 207.

7. Anonymous, "Tripping the Long, Hard Fantastic," p. 44.

8. Ibid.

9. Anonymous, "The Passing of 'The Giants' in the Women's Movement," *Literary Digest* 77/5 (5 May 1923): 46.

10. Nancy Cott, *The Groundings of Modern Feminism* (New Haven: Yale University Press, 1987), p. 5.

11. Ruth Mix, "Are Dance Marathons Dangerous?" *Journal of Social Hygiene* (March 1934): 169–70.

12. Edna Smith, interview with author, *New Observations* 39 (1986): 19.

13. Barbara Melosh, *Engendering Culture: Manhood and Womanhood in New Deal Public Art and Theater* (Washington, D.C.: Smithsonian Institution Press, 1991), p. 160.

14. Richard Elliott, interview with author, *New Observations* 39 (1986): 9.

15. Ibid.

16. George Eells, "Some 20,000 Were in 'Marathon Dance' Biz at Zenith of Craze," *Variety*, 7 January 1970, p. 154.

17. Anonymous, letter to author, 28 March 1985.

18. Kathy Peiss, *Cheap Amusements: Working Women and Leisure in Turn-of-the-Century New York* (Philadelphia: Temple University Press, 1986), p. 98.

19. Stan West, interview with author, Burbank, California, 22 May 1986.

20. Ibid.

21. Mix, "Are Dance Marathons Dangerous?" pp. 169–70.

22. Peiss, *Cheap Amusements*, p. 98.

23. Richard Kaplan, "An Appeal to Reason," *Billboard*, 29 June 1935, p. 31.

24. Banner, *Women in Modern America*, p. 153.

25. Melosh, *Engendering Culture*, p. 17.

26. Cott, *Groundings of Modern Feminism*, p. 3.

27. Horace McCoy, *They Shoot Horses, Don't They?* (New York: Avon Books, 1966), p. 94.

28. Ibid.

5. HAL J. ROSS: CUNNING, SMART, AND SLICK

1. Anonymous, *Billboard*, 25 August 1934.

2. Richard Elliott, interview with author, *New Observations* 39 (1986): 7.

3. "Marathon Entries Are Made Here in Last Several Days," *Texas South-Press*, 20 August 1930.

4. "Jazz Band Will Play Accompaniment as Tommy and Mary Are Married with Mock Ceremony at Dance Friday Night," unidentified news-clipping from the scrapbook of Richard Elliott.

5. "Strange Things Usually Happen in Marathon Dance, Director States," unidentified newsclipping from Elliott scrapbook.

6. Unidentified newsclipping from Elliott scrapbook.

7. "Human Interest Incidents of Long Endurance Stir Crowd; Marathon Set to End First Week Late Last Night," unidentified newsclipping from Elliott scrapbook.

8. "Corpus Christi Woman, Entrant in Marathon, Dances for 3 Days with Long Glass Sliver in Foot," unidentified newsclipping from Elliott scrapbook.

9. Ibid.

10. "Dancers Still Struggle for Prize Awards," unidentified newsclipping from Elliott scrapbook.

11. Hal J. Ross, "In the Training Quarters," *The Marathoner* (Canton, Ohio, 1929), p. 15.

12. "Snappy Orchestra Will Aid Dancers in Long Marathon, *Texas South-Press,* 20 August 1930.

13. Elliott, *New Observations* interview, p. 10.

14. Unidentified newsclipping from Elliott scrapbook.

15. "Chicago Blues Singer to Be at Marathon," unidentified newsclipping from Elliott scrapbook.

16. "Jazz Band Will Play Accompaniment as Tommy and Mary Are Married with Mock Ceremony at Dance Friday Night."

17. "Marathon Dance Couple to Wed," unidentified newsclipping from Elliott scrapbook.

18. "Gay Dancers Are Awarded Prize Money," unidentified newsclipping from Elliott scrapbook.

19. Elliott, *New Observations* interview, p. 7.

20. "Winning Name Chosen for Singer of Blues," *The Tampa Sunday Tribune,* 16 November 1930.

21. "S.R.O. Placard Is Hung as Crowd Crams Frolics," unidentified newsclipping from Elliott scrapbook.

22. "Few Hours Will Bring End to Long Marathon Dance with Two Couples Past 730-Hour Mark of Hard Fight," unidentified newsclipping from Elliott scrapbook.

23. "Marathon Dancers," *Valley Morning Star,* 27 June 1930.

24. "Soc 'n Club," *Galveston Daily News,* 20 October 1930.

25. "Wedding Rehearsal Marathon Feature," unidentified newsclipping from Elliott scrapbook.

26. "Bed-ridden Lad Is Cheered by Number," *Galveston Daily News,* 1 October 1930.

27. Elliott, *New Observations* interview, p.8.

28. Charles R. Mares, M.D., letter to Richard Elliott, 28 October 1930, Elliott scrapbook.

29. Charles Shea, [undated] letter to Richard Elliott, Elliott scrapbook.

30. E. L. Wall, letter to Richard Elliott, 28 October 1930, Elliott scrapbook.

31. Elliott, *New Observations* interview, p. 9.

32. Ibid., p. 8.

33. Ibid.

34. "Marathon Treasury Looted by Thieves," unidentified newsclipping from Elliott scrapbook.

35. "Marathon Dancers to Aid Miami Needy," *Miami Daily News,* 22 December 1930.

36. Ibid.

37. "Don't Bet on Jai Alai," *Miami Sports,* 28 December 1930.

38. "Brains Needed to Win Dance," unidentified newsclipping from Elliott scrapbook.

39. "Marathon to Help Legion," unidentified newsclipping from Elliott scrapbook.

40. Stan West, letter to author, 20 October 1990.

41. Elliott, *New Observations* interview, p. 10.

6. NATIONAL ENDURANCE AMUSEMENT ASSOCIATION

1. Jimmy Scott, "Is the Endurance Show Durable?" *Billboard,* 14 April 1934, p. 43.

2. Ibid.

3. Ibid.

4. Eddie Gilmartin, "Why a Successful Walkathon—Marathon?" *Billboard,* 30 June 1934, p. 25.

5. Hal J. Ross, "The Walkathon as a Business," *Billboard,* 25 August 1934, p. 43.

6. Ibid.

7. Richard S. Kaplan, "Protecting the Walkathon Promoter," *Billboard,* 20 October 1934, p. 26.

8. Richard S. Kaplan, "The Walkathon Future," *Billboard,* 1 December 1934, p. 27.

9. Ibid.

10. Ray C. Alvis, "Author Is in Favor of Organization," *Billboard,* 29 December 1934, p. 220.

11. Ibid.

12. Leo A. Seltzer, "What Future—Walkathons?" *Billboard,* 29 December 1934, p. 220.

13. Editorial, "Action," *Billboard,* 29 December 1934, p. 24.

14. Editorial, "Stalling," *Billboard,* 12 January 1935, p. 25.

15. Ibid.

16. Fredrick Lewis Allen, *Only Yesterday* (New York: Bonanza Books, 1986), p. 46.

17. Editorial, "On to Chicago," *Billboard,* 26 January 1935, p. 25.

18. Editorial, "Organization a Reality," *Billboard,* 9 February 1935, p. 26. The account of the organizational meeting in the following paragraphs is drawn from this editorial.

19. Editorial, "We're Facing a Test," *Billboard,* 22 February 1935, p. 23.

20. Charles Stephenson and Robert Asher, eds., *Life and Labor: Dimensions of American Working-Class History* (Albany: State University of New York Press, 1986), p. 5.

21. Edna Smith, interview with author, *New Observations* 39 (1986): 21.

22. Ibid.

23. Norma Jasper, letter to author, 1986.

24. Richard S. Kaplan, "Operators Need NEAA," *Billboard,* 16 March 1935, p. 25.

25. Ibid.

26. "Town Meeting Votes in Favor of Walkie," *Billboard,* 30 March 1935, p. 26.

27. "NEAA Victor in Calif. Fight," *Billboard,* 6 April 1935, p. 26.

28. "NEAA Takes Opening Battle; Seen as Operators Only Out," *Billboard,* 4 May 1935, p. 29.

29. Stew Allen, "Urges Laggers to Support of Endurance Org," *Billboard,* 5 October 1935, p. 28.

30. "NEAA Takes in Contestants," *Billboard,* 8 June 1935, p. 29.

31. Stan West, letter to author, 20 October 1990.

7. UNNEGOTIABLE REALITIES

1. Bascom Johnson, letter to chiefs of police, 24 February 1934, Library of Congress, Washington, D.C.

2. James McRell, letter to Bascom Johnson, 5 March 1934, Library of Congress, Washington, D.C.

3. Ms. [first name not known] Pinney and Mr. [first name not known] Kinsie, unpublished report, 24 April 1934, American Social Health Association records, University of Minnesota, Minneapolis.

4. Richard Kaplan, "Tidbits," *Billboard,* 28 December 1935.

5. Pennsylvania Act. No. 145, Sessions Laws of 1931.

6. Anonymous, article in *Journal of Social Hygiene* 21 (October–November 1925): 369.

7. American Legislator's Association, collected marathon dance laws.

8. Indiana Chapter No. 28, approved 6 February 1935.

9. Joan M. Crouse, *The Homeless Transient in the Great Depression* (Albany: State University of New York Press, 1986).

10. Kaplan, "Tidbits," *Billboard,* 19 October 1935, p. 28.

11. Ibid.

12. Ibid.

13. Kaplan, "Tidbits," *Billboard,* 26 October 1935, p. 34.

14. Kaplan, "Tidbits," *Billboard,* 2 November 1935, p. 27.

15. Kaplan, *Billboard,* 31 August 1935, p. 34.

16. Kaplan, "Tidbits," *Billboard,* 26 October 1935, p. 34.

17. Kaplan, "Tidbits," *Billboard,* 2 November 1935, p. 27.

18. Kaplan, "Tidbits," *Billboard,* 9 November 1935, p. 28.

19. Kaplan, "Tidbits," *Billboard,* 16 November 1935, p. 27.

20. Kaplan, "Tidbits," *Billboard,* 9 November 1935, p. 28.

21. Stan West, interview with author, Burbank, California, 22 May 1986.

22. Kaplan, "Tidbits," *Billboard,* 9 November 1935, p. 28; 14 December 1935, p. 28; 28 December 1935, p. 80.

23. Kaplan, "Tidbits," *Billboard,* 28 December 1935, p. 80.

24. Kaplan, "Tidbits," *Billboard,* 16 November 1935, p. 27.

25. Kaplan, "Tidbits," *Billboard,* 21 December 1935, p. 29.

26. Ibid.

27. Kaplan, "Tidbits," *Billboard,* 7 December 1935, p. 27.

28. Kaplan, "Tidbits," *Billboard,* 28 December 1935, p. 80.

29. Kaplan, "Tidbits," *Billboard,* 18 April 1936, p. 27.

30. Ibid.

31. Don King, article in *Billboard,* 4 April 1936, p. 26.

32. Kaplan, "Tidbits," *Billboard,* 25 April 1936, p. 27.

33. Kaplan, "Tidbits," *Billboard,* 22 August 1936, p. 70.

34. Susan Ware, *Holding Their Own* (Boston: Twayne, 1982), p. 171.

Sources

PRIMARY SOURCES

Interviews

Bergman, Raja. Interview with author. Van Nuys, California, 31 May 1986.
Eells, George. Interview with author. *New Observations* 39 (1986).
———. Interview with author. New York City, 7 August 1985.
———. Interview with author. Hollywood, California, 16 April 1986.
———. Interview with author. New York City, 18 September 1986.
Elliott, Richard. Interview with author. *New Observations* 39 (1986).
———. Interview with author. San Bernalillo, New Mexico, 4 April 1985.
Jasper, Norma. Interview with author. Van Nuys, California, 15 May 1986.
Meyer, Betty. Interview with author. *New Observations* 39 (1986).
Smith, Edna. Interview with author. *New Observations* 39 (1986).
———. Telephone interview with author. 19 March 1985.
West, Stan. Interview with author. Burbank, California, 22 May 1986.

Letters

Anonymous. Letter to author. 28 March 1985.
Calabria, Frank. Letter to author. 29 April 1985.
Cook, George. Letter to author. 4 April 1985.
Eells, George. Letter to author. 10 November 1984.
———. Letter to author. 23 April 1986.
Elliott, Richard. Letter to author. 10 November 1984.
———. Letter to author. 3 June 1985.
———. Letter to author. 13 November 1986.
———. Letter to author. 22 March 1987.
———. Letter to author. 19 February 1989.

Foster, Walter. Letter to author. 4 December 1984.

Freund, Betty. Letter to author. 2 November 1985.

Gorley, Robert. Letter to author. 8 December 1984.

———. Letter to author. 9 April 1985.

Jasper, Norma. Letter to author. 1986.

Johnson, Bascom. Letter to chiefs of police. 24 February 1934. Library of Congress, Washington, D.C.

Mares, Charles R. Letter to Richard Elliott. 28 October 1930. Collection of Richard Elliott.

McRell, James. Letter to Bascom Johnson. 5 March 1934. Library of Congress, Washington, D.C.

Meyer, Betty. Letter to author. 1 November 1984.

———. Letter to author. 30 May 1985.

Outland, Orland. Letter to author. 2 November 1984.

Perlman, Everett. Letter to author. 22 October 1986.

Ritoff, Mike J. Letter to author. 8 July 1986.

Rothman, June. Letter to author. 21 February 1986.

Shea, Charles. Letter to Richard Elliott. N.d. Collection of Richard Eliott.

Smith, Edna. Letter to author. 4 November 1984.

———. Letter to author. 11 May 1985.

Surut, Jack. Letter to author. 30 October 1984.

Wall, E. L. Letter to Richard Elliott. 28 October 1930.

West, Stan. Letter to author. 23 March 1990.

———. Letter to author. 20 October 1990.

Magazines and Journals

Allen, Stew. "Urges Laggers to Support of Endurance Org." *Billboard* (5 October 1935).

Alvis, Ray C. "Author Is in Favor of Organization." *Billboard* (8 December 1988).

Anonymous. Editorial. "Action." *Billboard* (29 December 1934).

———. Editorial. "On to Chicago." *Billboard* (26 January 1935).

———. Editorial. "Organization a Reality." *Billboard* (9 February 1935).

———. Editorial. "Stalling." *Billboard* (12 January 1935).

———. Editorial. "The Turning Point." *Billboard* (19 January 1935).

———. Editorial. "We're Facing a Test." *Billboard* (22 February 1935).

———. "NEAA Takes in Contestants." *Billboard* (8 June 1935).

———. "NEAA Takes Opening Battle; Seen as Operators Only 'Out'." *Billboard* (4 May 1935).

———. "NEAA Victor in Calif. Fight." *Billboard* (6 April 1935).

———. "Town Meeting Votes in Favor of Walkie." *Billboard* (30 March 1935).

———. "Tripping the Long, Hard Fantastic for a Record." *The Literary Digest* 77/5 (5 May 1923).

Gilmartin, Eddie. "Why a Successful Walkathon—Marathon?" *Billboard* (30 June 1934).

Gingrich, Arnold. "Poor Man's Night Club." *Esquire* (Autumn 1933).

Kaplan, Richard. "An Appeal to Reason." *Billboard* (29 June 1935).

———. "Operators Need NEAA." *Billboard* (16 March 1935).

———. "Protecting the Walkathon Promoter." *Billboard* (20 October 1934).

———. "Tidbits." *Billboard* (31 August 1935).

———. "Tidbits." *Billboard* (19 October 1935).

———. "Tidbits." *Billboard* (26 October 1935).

———. "Tidbits." *Billboard* (2 November 1935).

———. "Tidbits." *Billboard* (9 November 1935).

———. "Tidbits." *Billboard* (16 November 1935).

———. "Tidbits." *Billboard* (7 December 1935).

———. "Tidbits." *Billboard* (14 December 1935).

———. "Tidbits." *Billboard* (21 December 1935).

———. "Tidbits." *Billboard* (28 December 1935).

———. "Tidbits." *Billboard* (4 April 1936).

———. "Tidbits." *Billboard* (11 April 1936).

———. "Tidbits." *Billboard* (18 April 1936).

———. "Tidbits." *Billboard* (25 April 1936).

———. "Tidbits." *Billboard* (22 August 1936).

———. "The Walkathon Future." *Billboard* (1 December 1934).

Kaye, Joseph. "Dance of Fools." *Dance Magazine* (February 1931): 12–13; continues on 54.

Mix, Ruth. "Are Dance Marathons Dangerous?" *Journal of Social Hygiene* (March 1934).

Ross, Hal J. "Is the Endurance Show Durable?" *Billboard* (14 April 1934).

———. "The Walkathon as a Business." *Billboard* (25 August 1934).

Seltzer, Leo. "What Future—Walkathons?" *Billboard* (29 December 1934).

Stein, Harold. "Dance Marathons: Look Back in Horror." *Dance Magazine* (February 1970): 68–71.

Newspapers

Anonymous. "Bed-ridden Lad Is Cheered by Number." *Galveston Daily News* (1 October 1930).

————. "Brains Needed to Win Dance."

————. "Chicago Blues Singer to Be at Marathon."

————. "Corpus Christi Woman, Entrant in Marathon, Dances for 3 Days with Long Glass Sliver in Foot."

————. "Dancers Still Struggle for Prize Awards."

————. "Don't Bet on Jai Alai." *Miami Sports* (28 December 1930).

————. "Gay Dancers Are Awarded Prize Money."

————. "Human Interest Incidents of Long Endurance Stir Crowd; Marathon Set to End First Week Late Last Night."

————. "Jazz Band Will Play Accompaniment as Tommy and Mary are Married with Mock Ceremony at Dance Friday Night."

————. "Marathon Dance Couple to Wed."

————. "Marathon Dance Gets Underway." *Galveston Daily News* (19 September 1930).

————. "Marathon Dancers." *Valley Morning Star* (Harlingen, Texas) (27 June 1930).

————. "Marathon Dancers to Aid Miami Needy." *Miami Daily News* (22 December 1930).

————. "Marathon Entries Are Made Here in Last Several Days." *Texas South-Press* (20 August 1930).

————. "Marathon to Help Legion."

————. "Marathon Treasury Looted by Thieves."

————. "Myrtle Fultz Drops Out of Hard Contest."

————. "Snappy Orchestra Will Aid Dancers in Long Marathon." *Texas South-Press* (20 August 1930).

————. "Soc 'n Club." *Galveston Daily News* (20 October 1930).

————. "S.R.O. Placard is Hung as Crowd Crams Frolics."

————. "Strange Things Usually Happen in Marathon Dance, Director States."

————. "Wedding Rehearsal Marathon Feature."

————. "Winning Name Chosen for Singer of Blues." *Tampa Sunday Tribune* (16 November 1930).

Nation (23 July 1928).

New York Times (2 April 1923–22 June 1928).

Pamphlets and Reports

Perlman, Everett, and Nelson, G. W. *The Marathon Guide.* Minneapolis: Privately printed, 1928.

[Ms.] Pinney [no first name given] and [Mr.] Kinsie [no first name given]. Unpublished report, 24 April 1934. In legal reference files section of the records of the American Social Health Association, University of Minnesota, Minneapolis.

Ross, Hal J. "In the Training Quarters." *The Marathoner.* Canton, Ohio, 1929.

Scrapbooks

Eells, George. Assorted photographic scrapbooks. Collection of George Eells.

Elliott, Richard. Photographs and clippings of Hal J. Ross's American marathons. Collection of Richard Elliott.

———. Photographs and clippings of Hal J. Ross's European marathons. Collection of Richard Elliott.

Matthews, Lawrence. Clippings scrapbook. The Dance Collection, New York Public Library.

———. Photograph scrapbook. The Dance Collection, New York Public Library.

West, Stan. Photograph scrapbook of Snozzle Roth. Collection of Stan West.

SECONDARY SOURCES

Articles

Calabria, Frank M. "The Dance Marathon Craze." *Journal of Popular Culture* 10 (Summer 1976): 54–69.

Eells, George. "Some 20,000 Were in 'Marathon Dance' Biz at Zenith of Craze." *Variety* (7 January 1970): 154.

Jameson, Frederic. "Reification and Utopia in Mass Culture." *Social Text* 1 (1979).

Morse, Margaret. "The Television News Personality and Credibility: Reflections on the News in Translation." In Tania Modleski, ed., *Studies in Entertainment* (1986), 55–79.

Scott, Jimmy. "We Danced All Night—And All Day!" *Ballroom Dance Magazine* (July 1961): 8–9, 20–24.

Books

Allen, Frederick Lewis. *Since Yesterday.* New York: Bonanza Books, 1986.

Banner, Lois. *Women in Modern America: A Brief History.* New York: Harcourt Brace Jovanovich, 1984.

Cott, Nancy F. *The Groundings of Modern Feminism.* New Haven: Yale University Press, 1987.

Crouse, Joan. *The Homeless Transient in the Great Depression*. Albany: State University of New York Press, 1986.

Erenberg, Lewis A. *Steppin' Out: New York Nightlife and the Transformation of American Culture*. Chicago: University of Chicago Press, 1981.

Garraty, John. *The Great Depression*. New York: Anchor Books, 1987.

Green, Abel, and Joe Laurie, Jr. *From Vaude to Video*. New York: Henry Holt, 1951.

Havoc, June. *Early Havoc*. New York: Simon and Schuster, 1959.

————. *More Havoc*. New York: Harper and Row, 1980.

Kessner, Thomas. *Fiorello H. La Guardia*. New York: Penguin Books, 1989.

Leuchtenburg, William. *The Perils of Prosperity 1914–32*. Chicago: University of Chicago Press, 1958.

McCoy, Horace. *They Shoot Horses, Don't They?* New York: Avon Books, 1935.

McElvaine, Robert. *The Great Depression*. New York: Times Books, 1984.

Melosh, Barbara. *Engendering Culture: Manhood and Womanhood in New Deal Public Art and Theater*. Washington: Smithsonian Institution Press, 1991.

Mertz, Charles. *The Great American Bandwagon*. New York: The Literary Guild of America, 1928.

Modleski, Tania. *Loving with a Vengeance*. New York: Methuen, 1984.

O'Day, Anita. *High Times Hard Times*. New York: G. P. Putnam, 1981.

Peiss, Kathy. *Cheap Amusements: Working Women and Leisure in Turn-of-the-Century New York*. Philadelphia: Temple University Press, 1986.

Sann, Paul. *Fads, Follies and Delusions*. New York: Henry Holt, 1959.

Shirley, Glenn. *"Hello Suckers!": The Story of Texas Guinan*. Austin: Eakin Press, 1989.

Stearns, Jean, and Marshall Stearns. *Jazz Dance*. New York: Schirmer Books, 1968.

Stephenson, Charles, and Robert Asher, eds. *Life and Labor: Dimensions of American Working-Class History*. Albany: State University of New York Press, 1986.

Susman, Warren. *Culture as History*. New York: Pantheon Books, 1984.

Ware, Susan. *Holding Their Own*. Boston: Twayne, 1982.

Weinstein, James. *The Corporate Ideal in the Liberal State 1900–1918*. Boston, Beacon Press, 1968.

Plays

Eells, George. *The Glory Walk*. Unpublished. Performing Arts Library, Lincoln Center, New York.

Havoc, June. *Marathon '33*. New York: Dramatists Play Service, 1969.

Index